The Little Book of Plotting
月刊三

This book is an artistic portfolio of my art done between 2016 and 2021, and consist of some of the pieces I am most please with, proud of, or otherwise my various favorites for various reasons. Also, since this is a portfolio of lineart, this portfolio also serves as a coloring book for the reader's added personal enjoyment.

Furthermore, I, the artist claim copyright of all art featured in this book, though I officially grant permission for personal or non-commercial use copies to be made. Other inquiries can be made to me via either apokryltaros@gmail.com or stanton.fink@protonmail.com

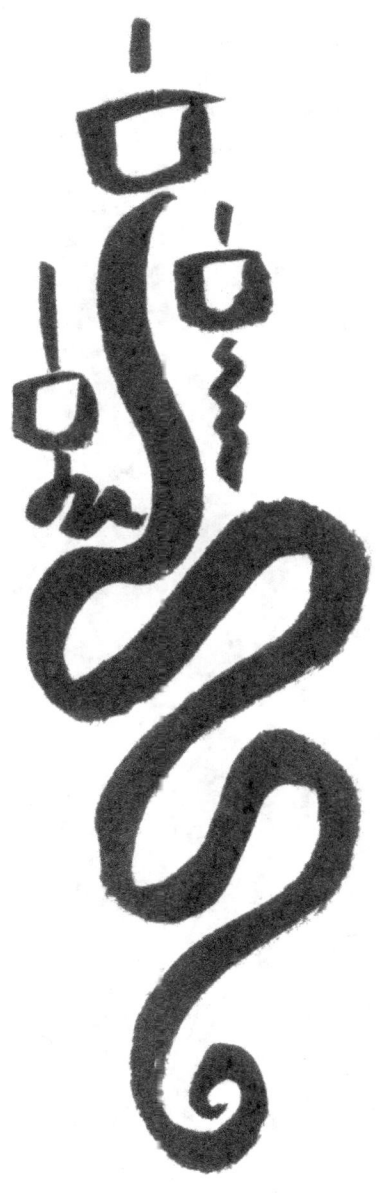

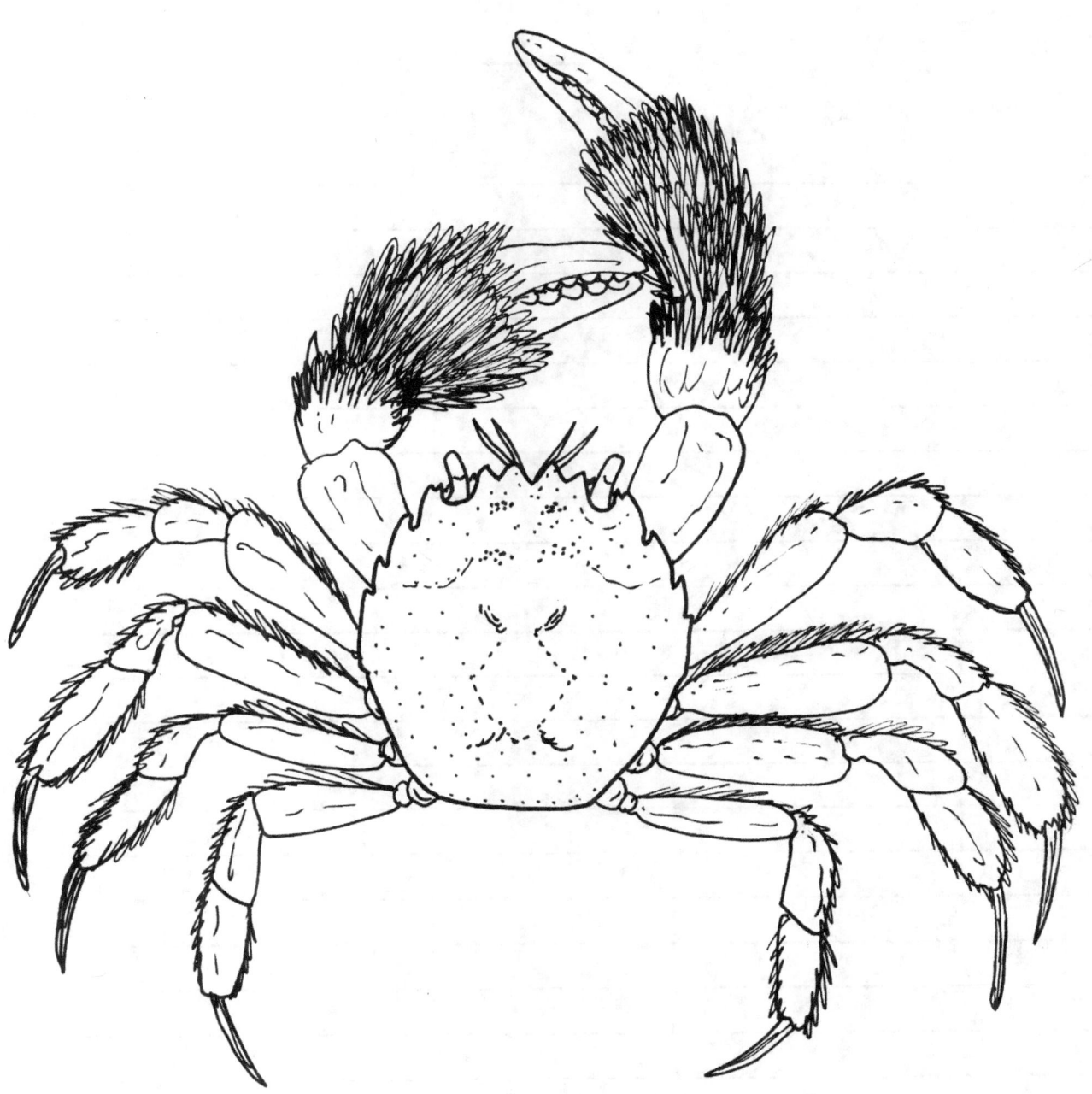

Eriocheir sinensis

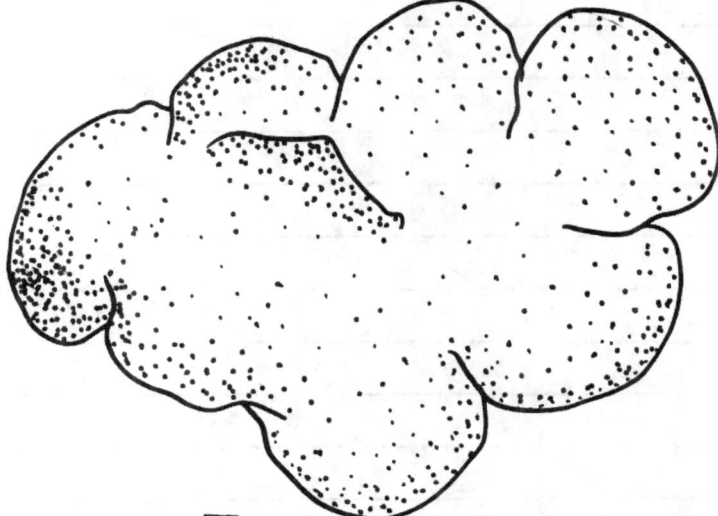
Tuber magnatum

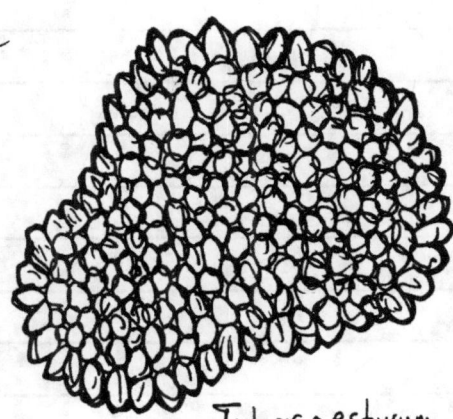
Tuber aestivum

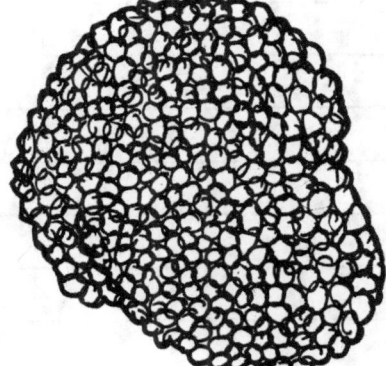
Tuber sinense

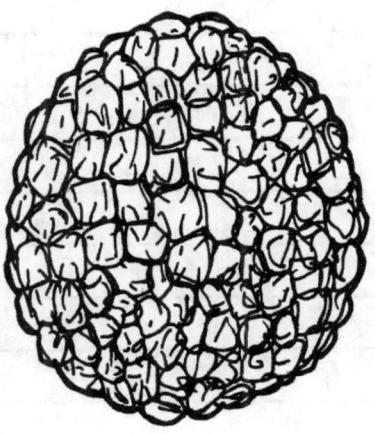
Tuber melanosporum

二

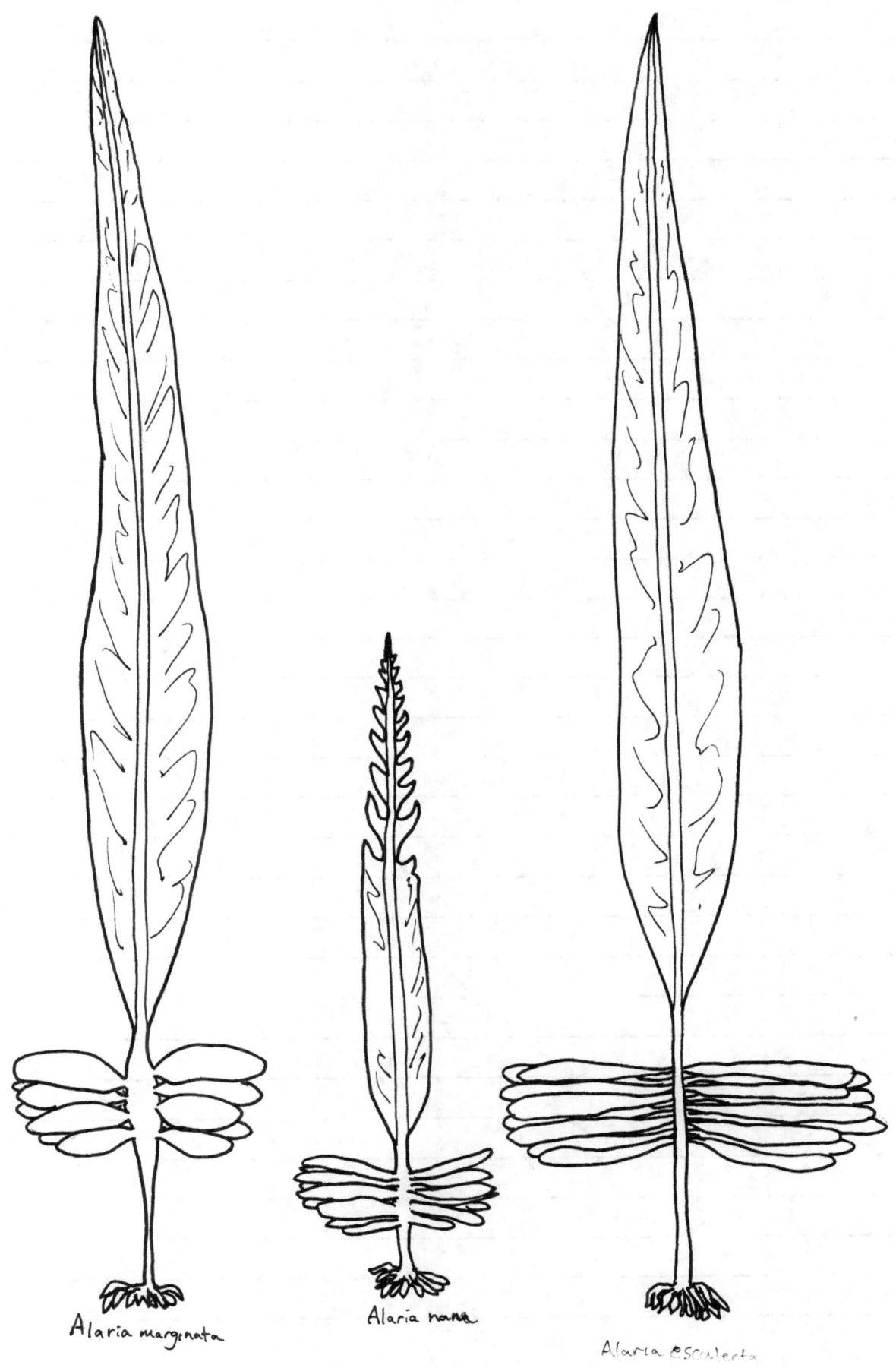

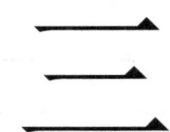

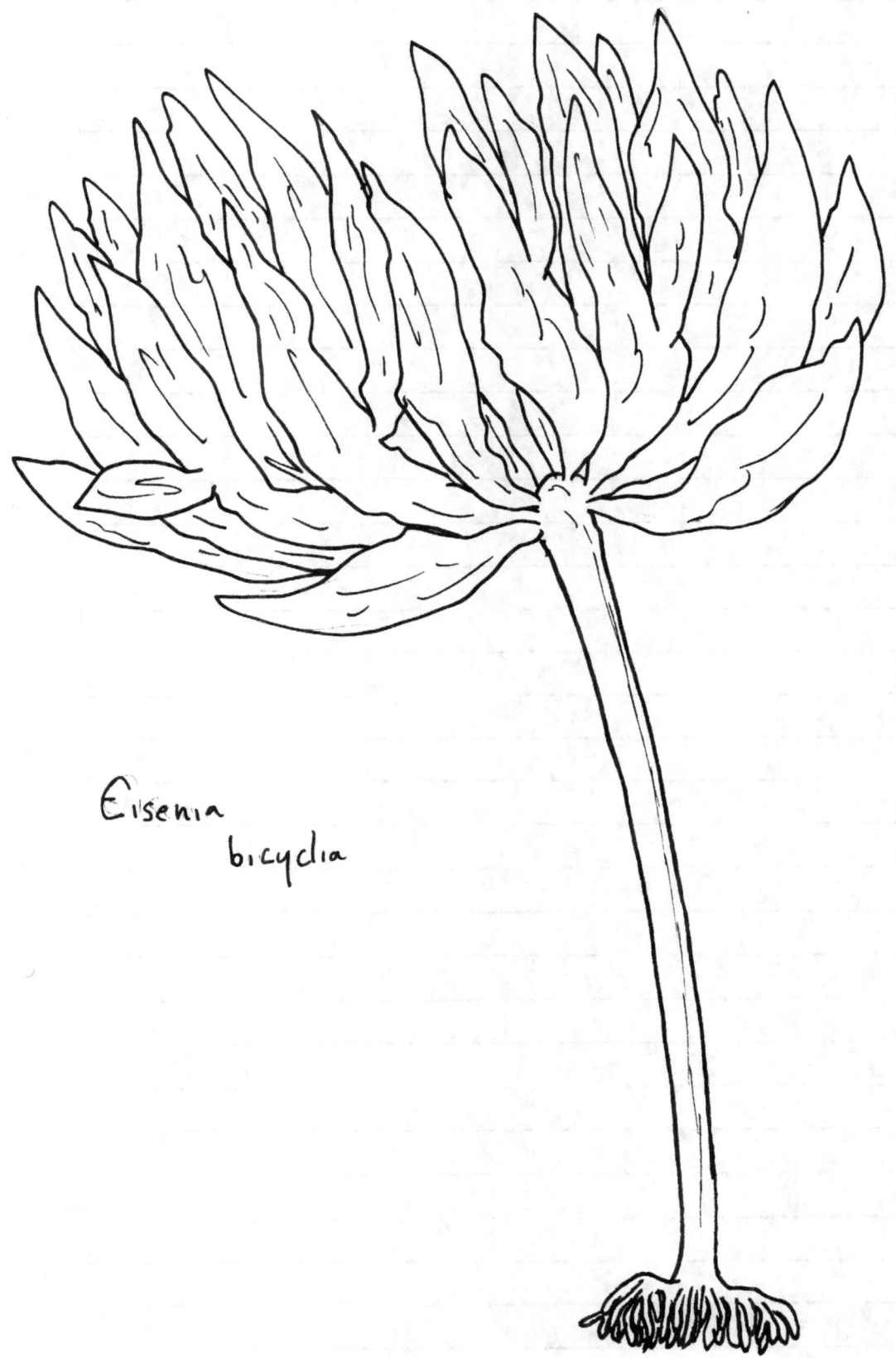

Eisenia bicyclia

四

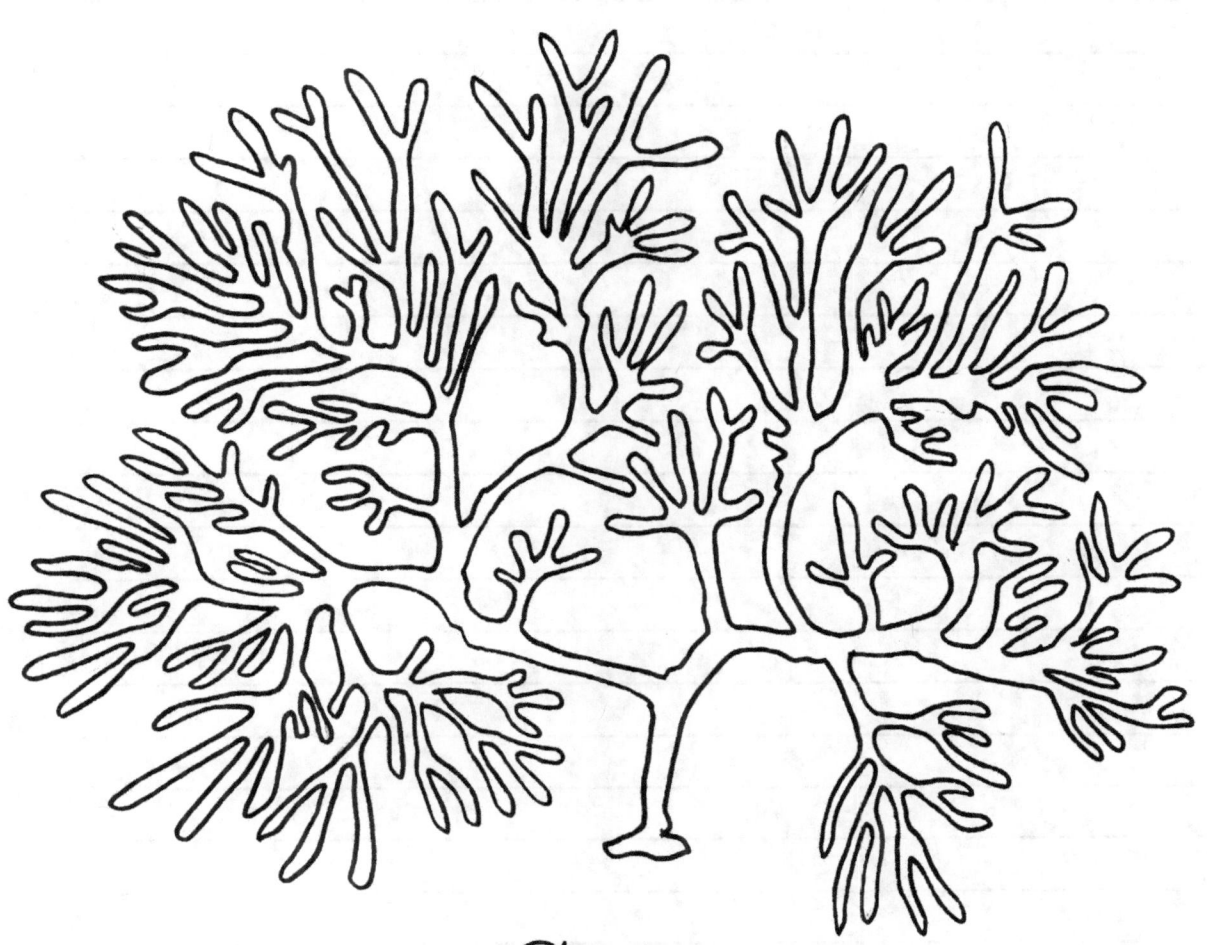

五

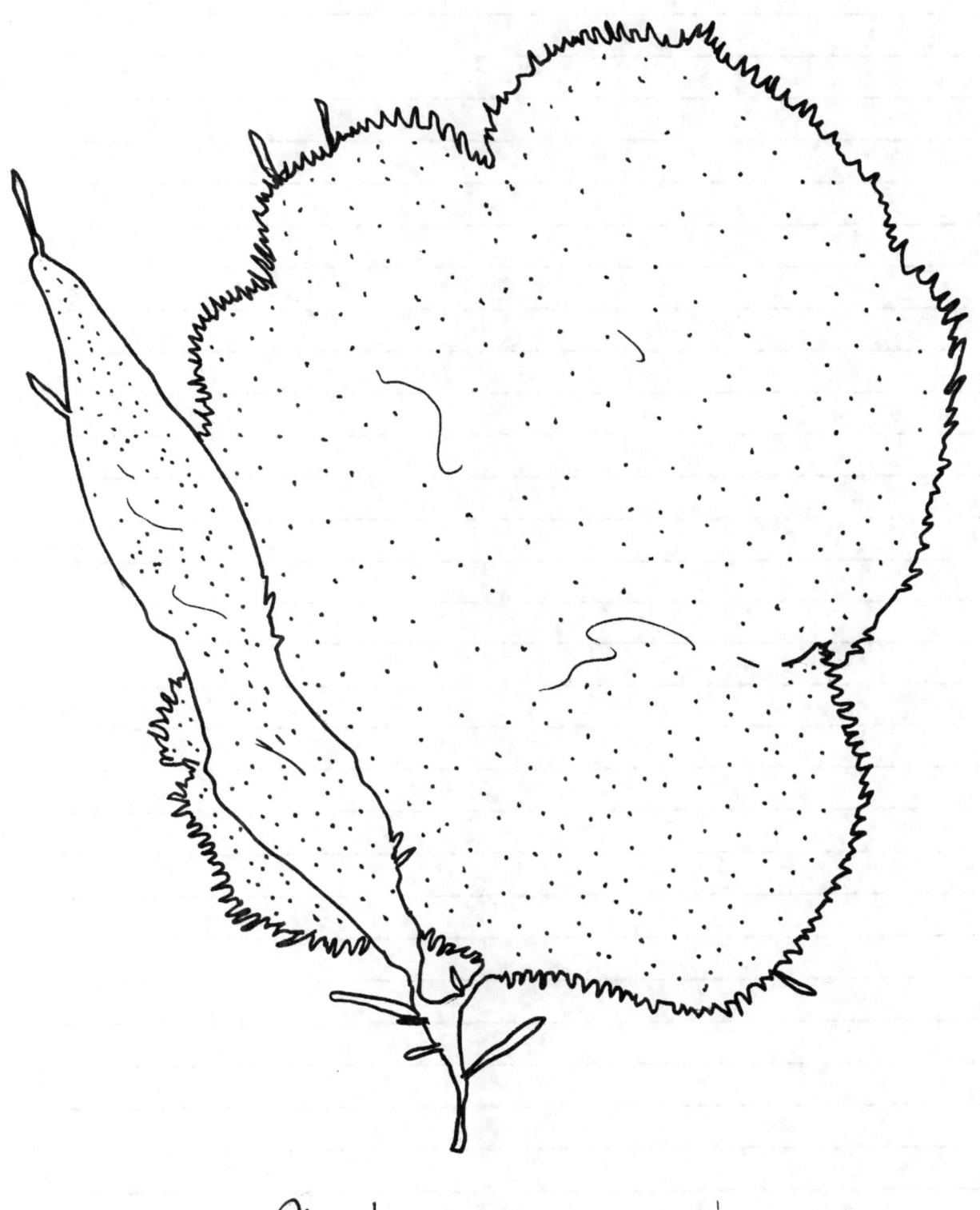

Chondracanthus exasperatus

六

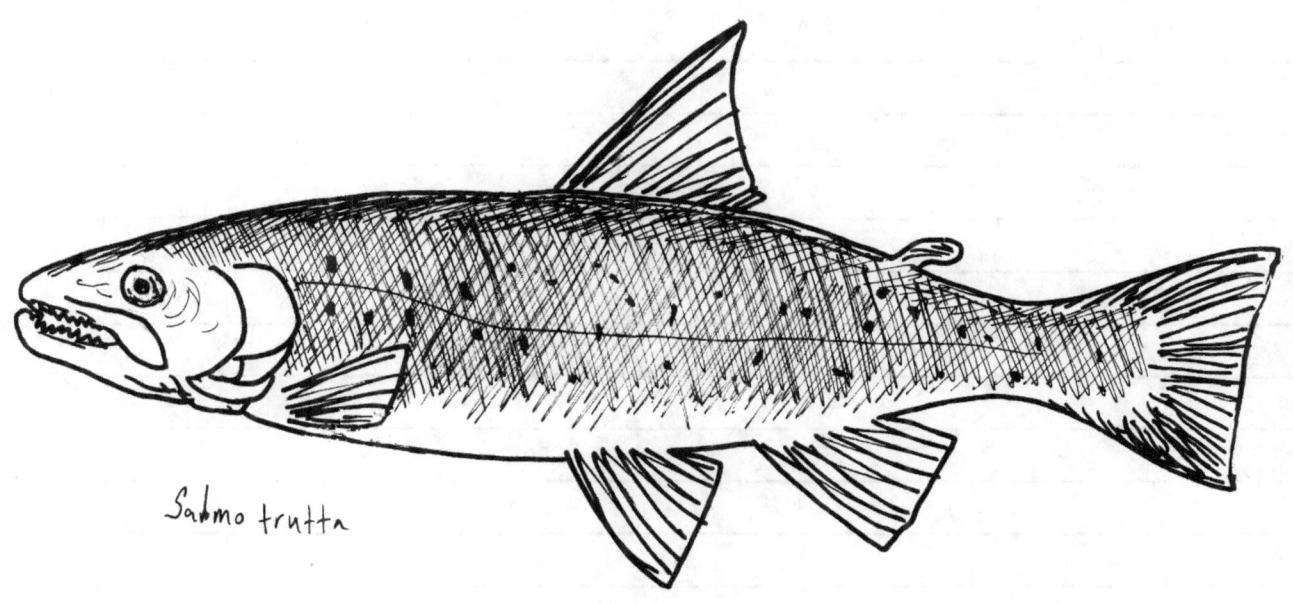

Salmo trutta

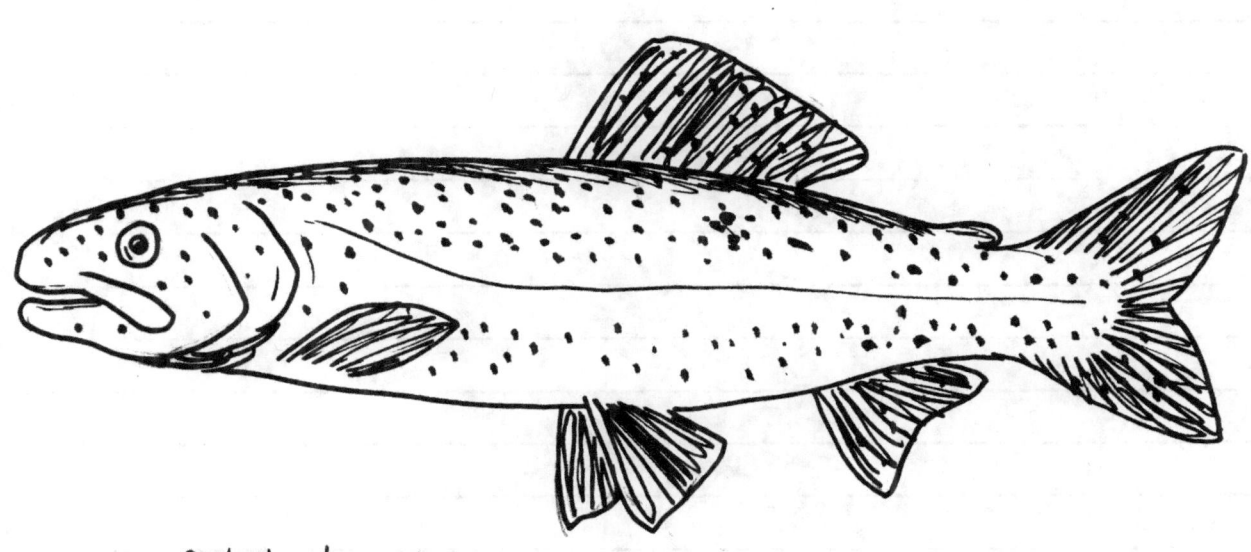

Onchorhynchus mykiss

七

Saccharina japonica

八

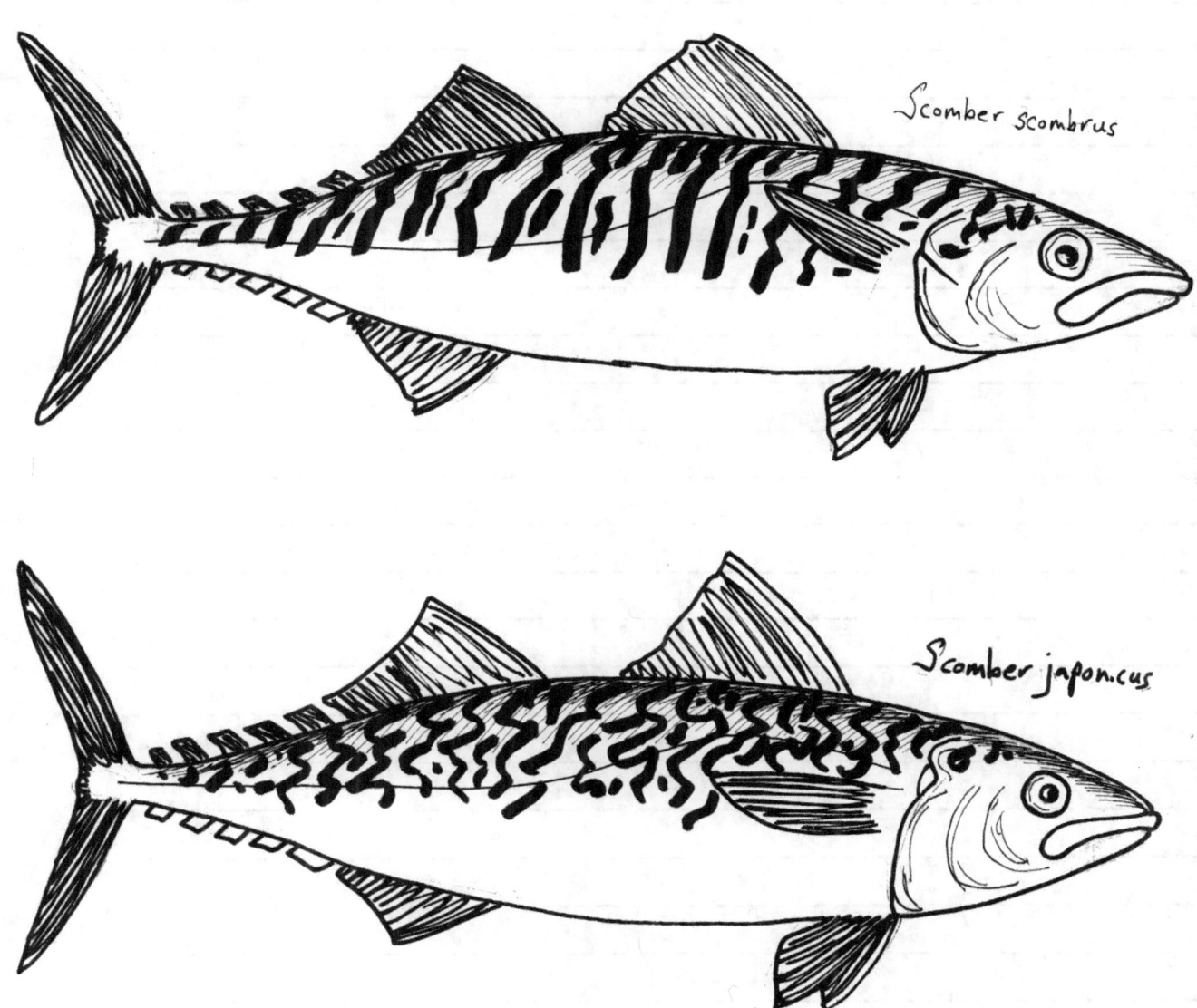

九

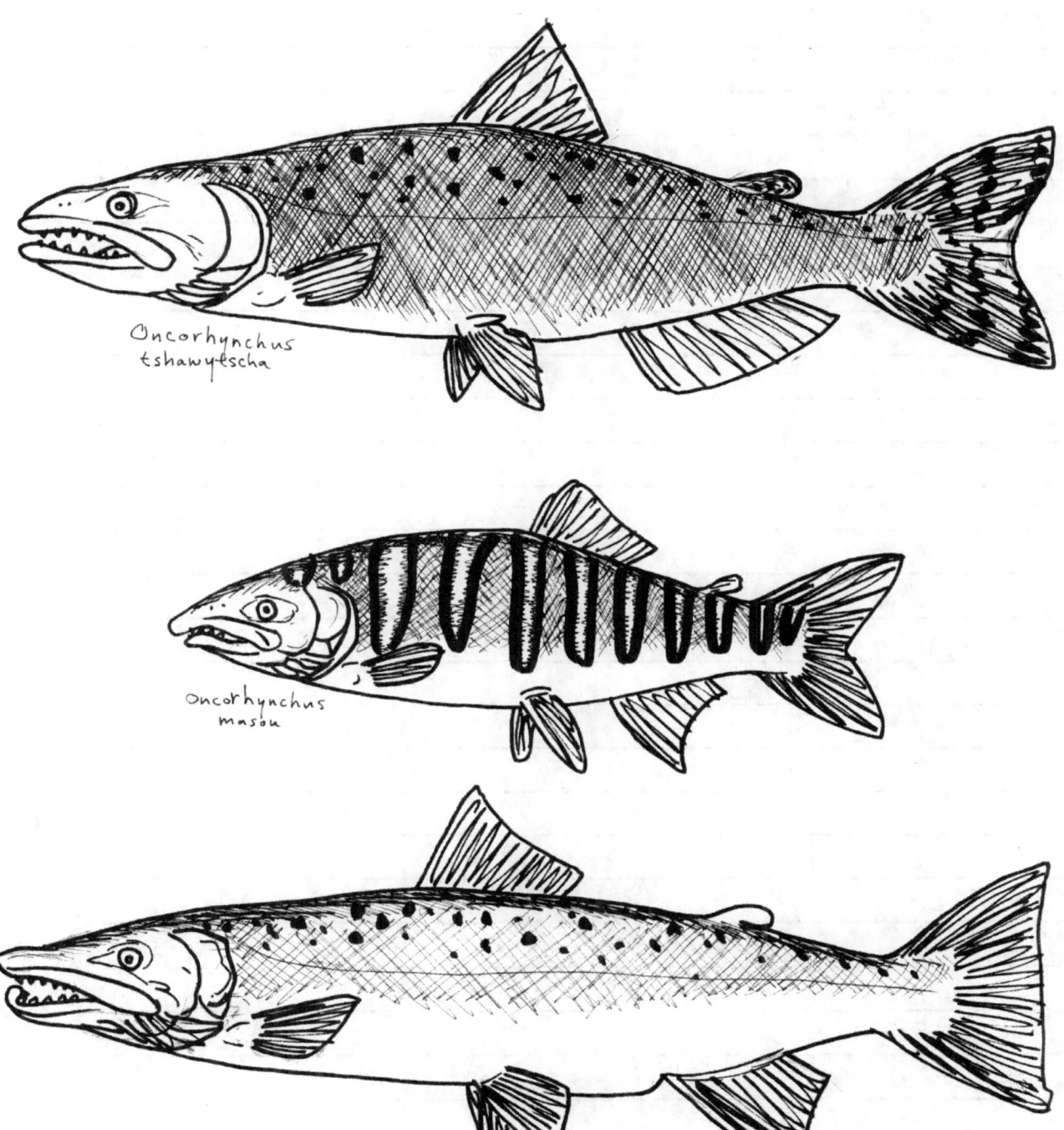

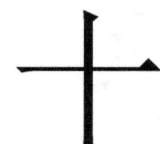

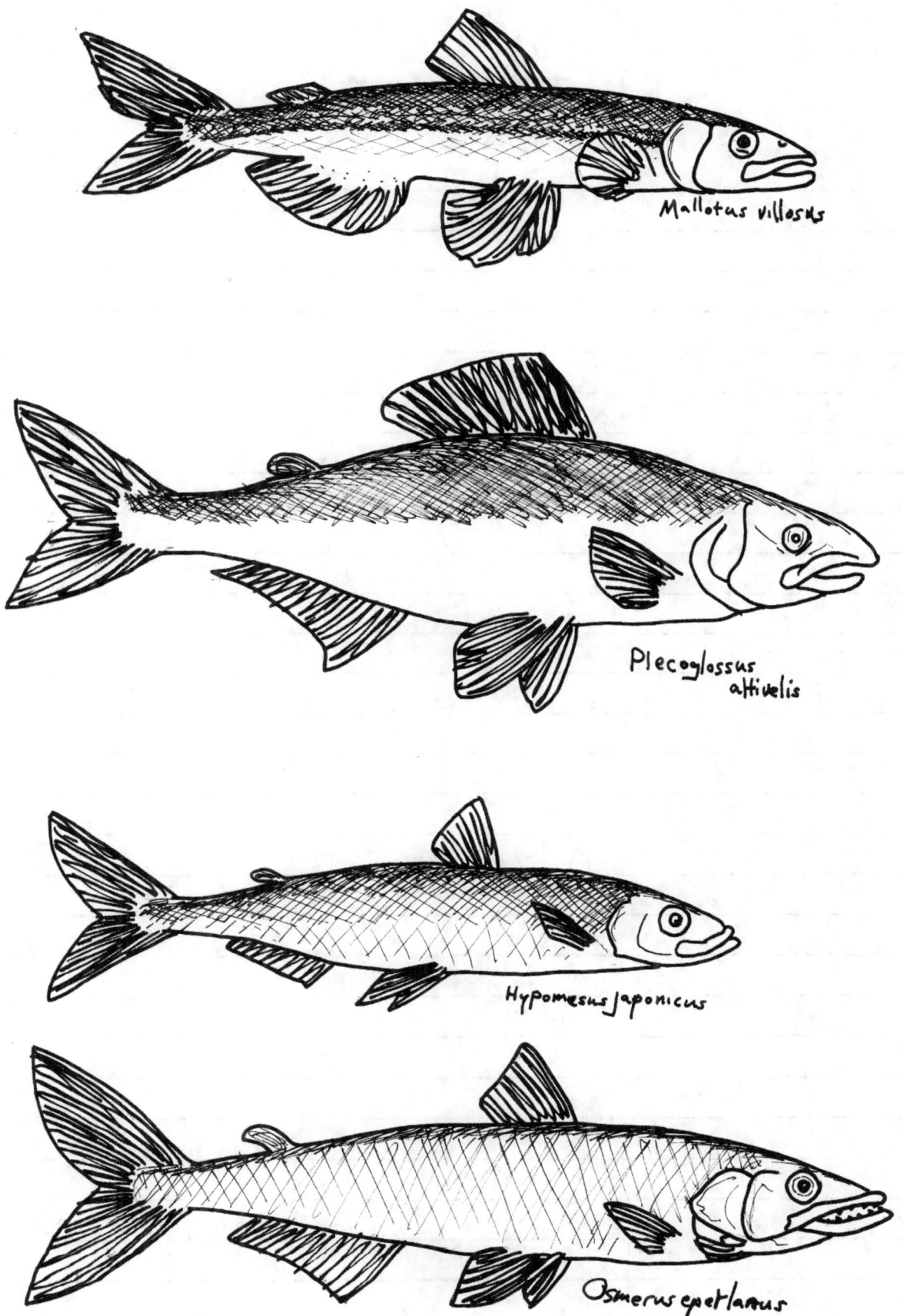

十一

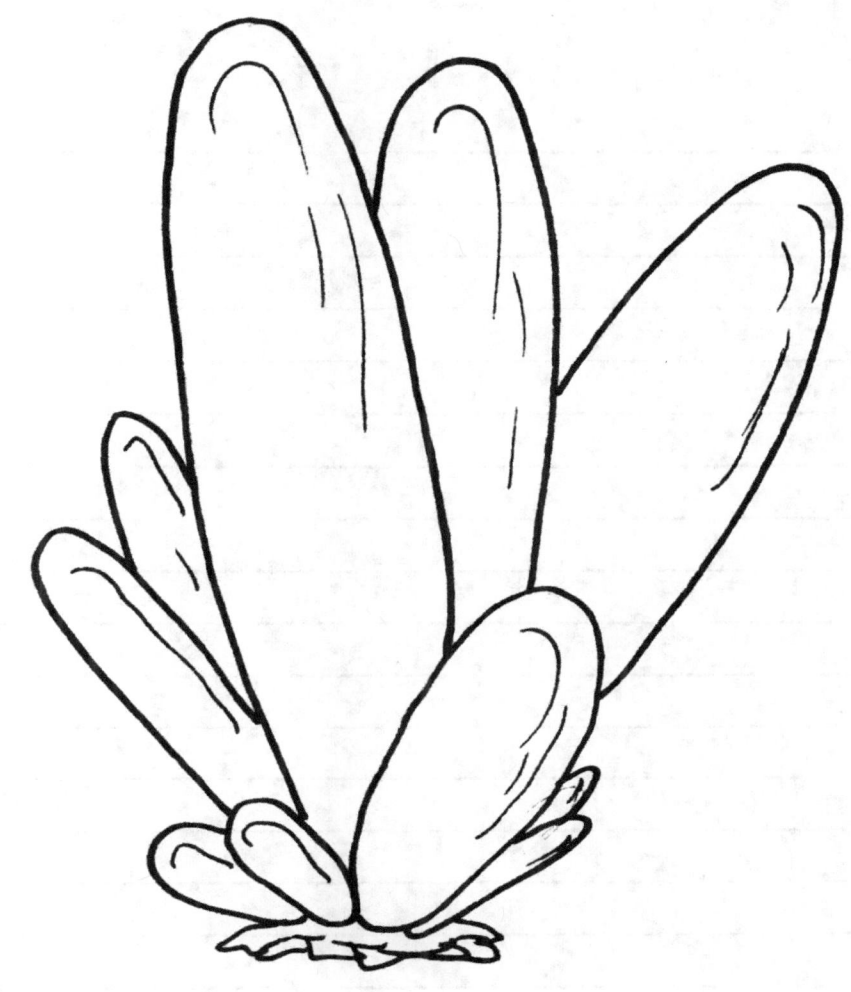

Halosaccion glandiforme

十二

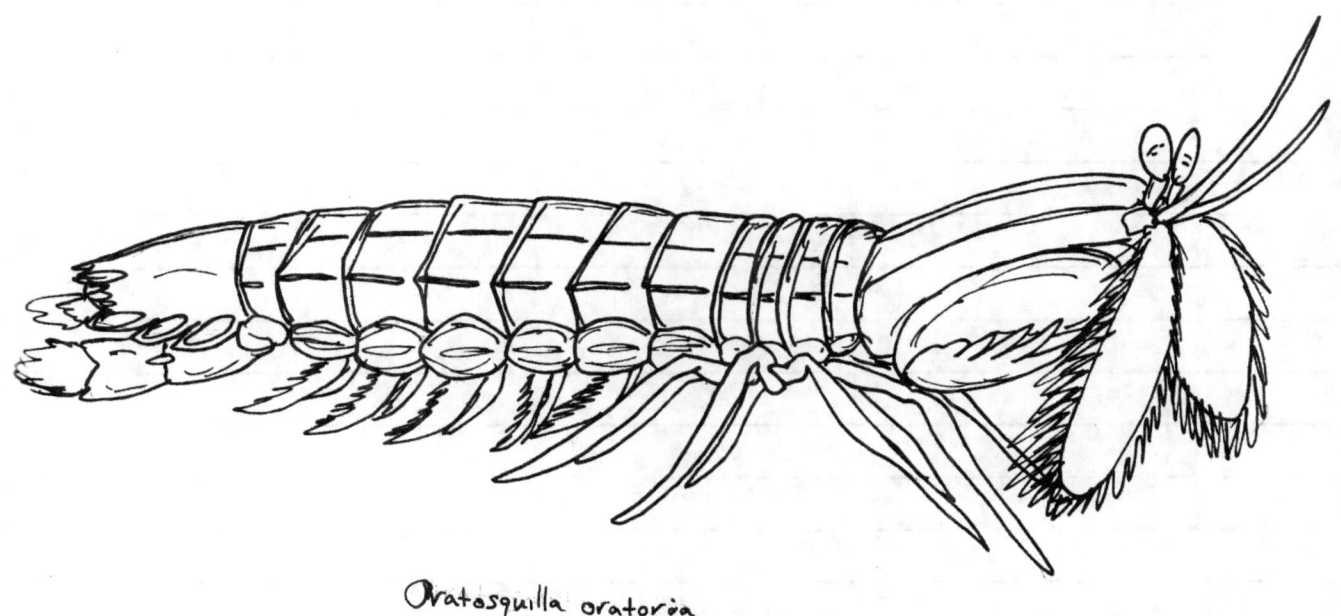
Oratosquilla oratoria

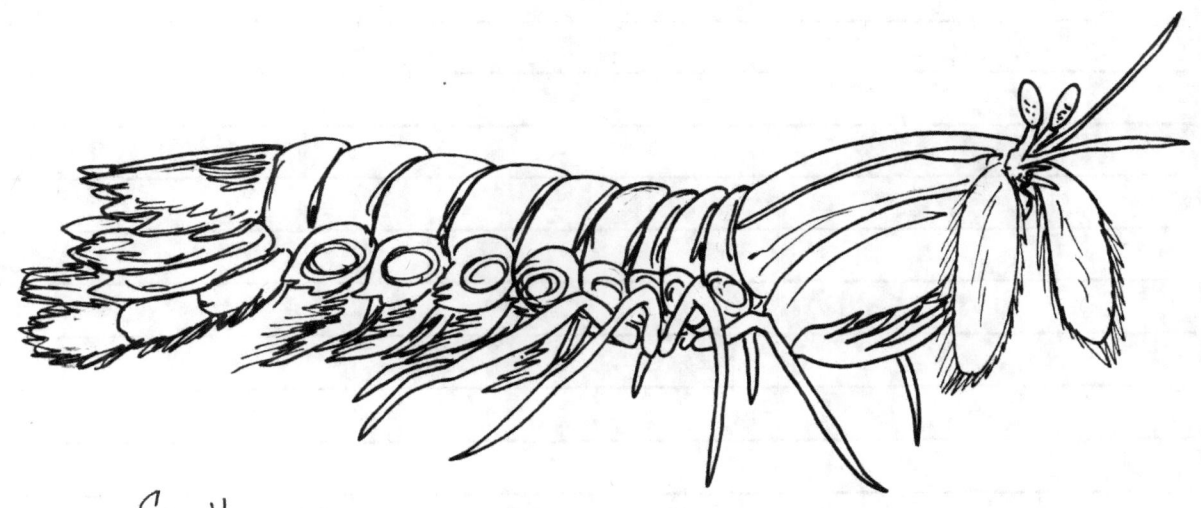
Squilla mantis

十三

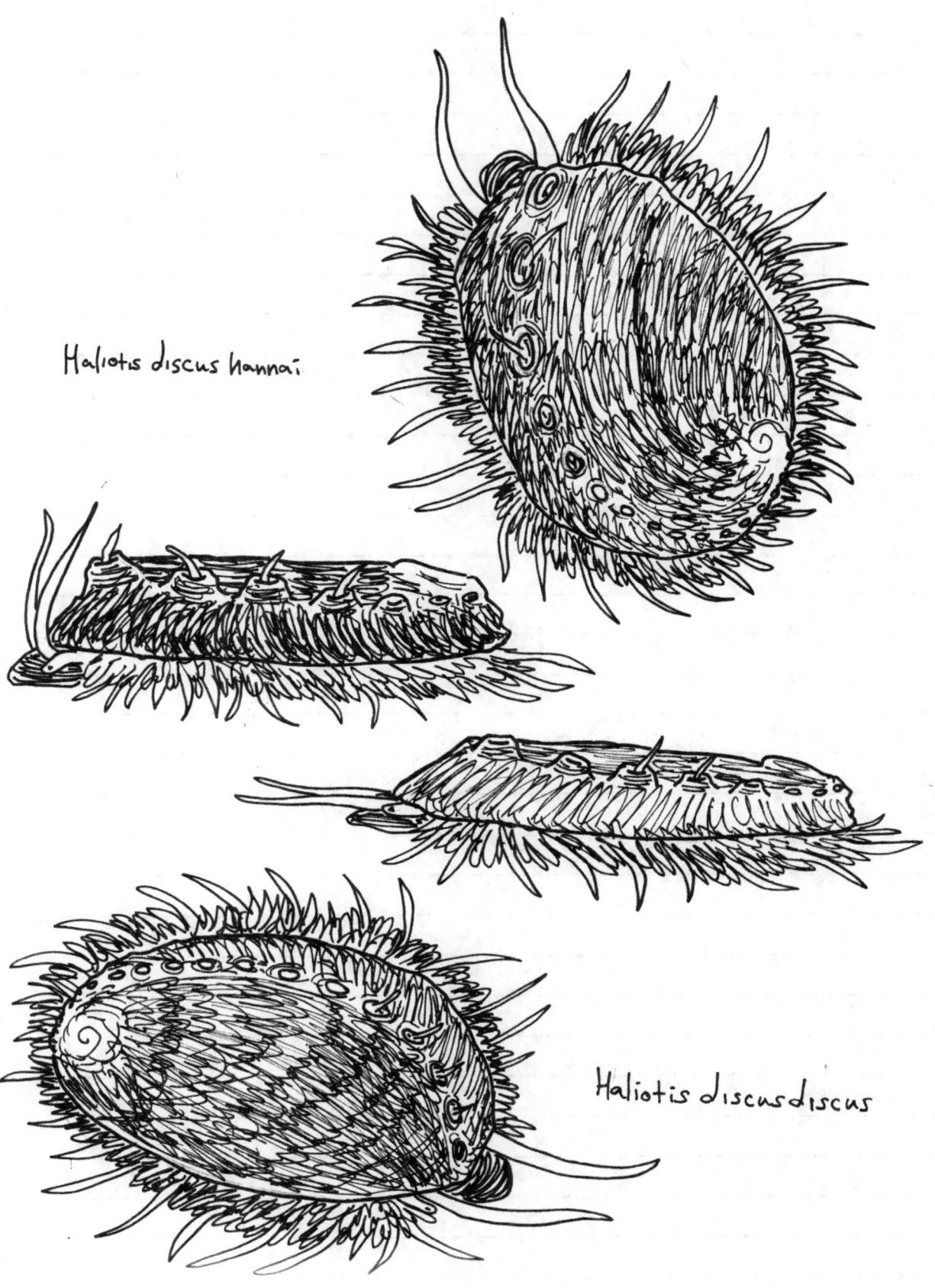

十四

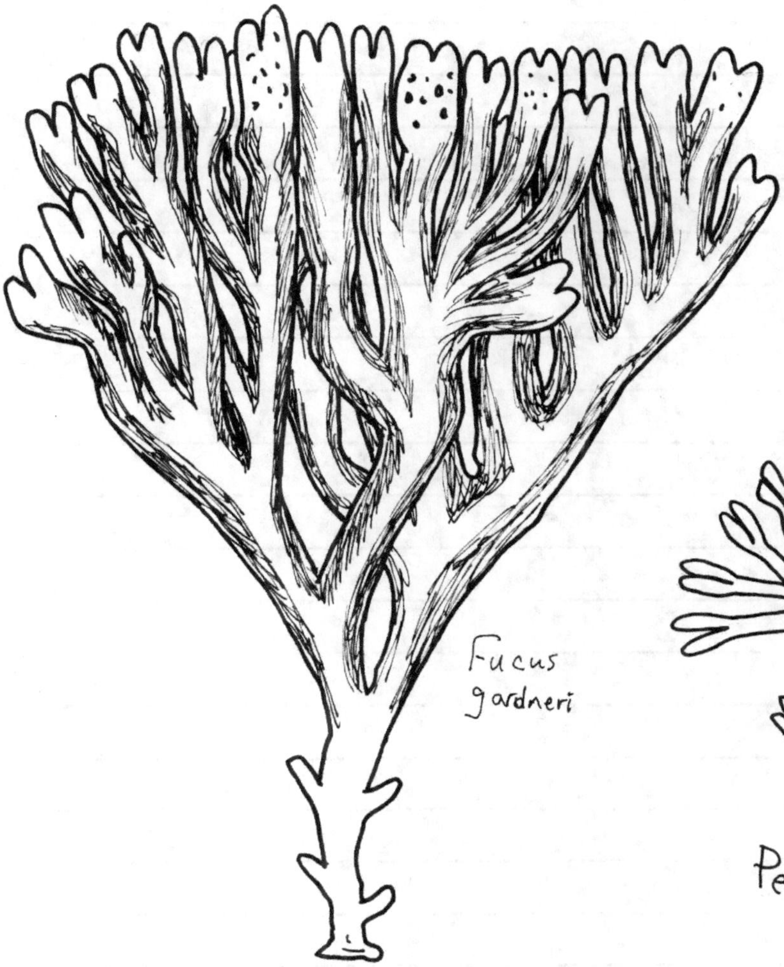

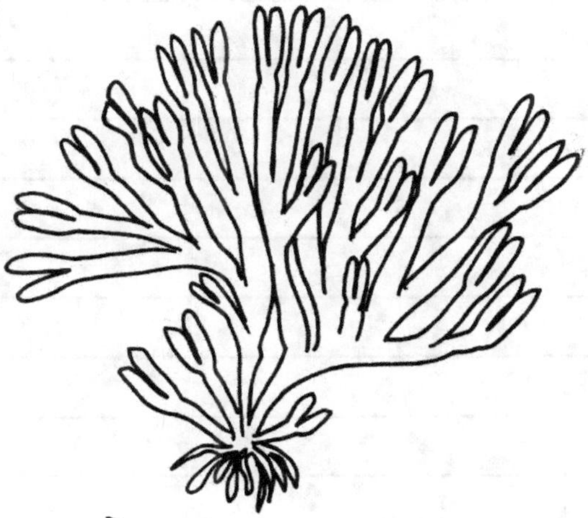

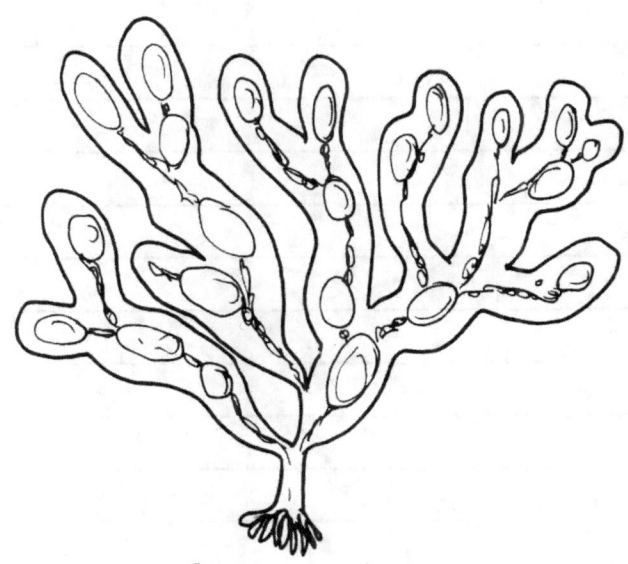

十五

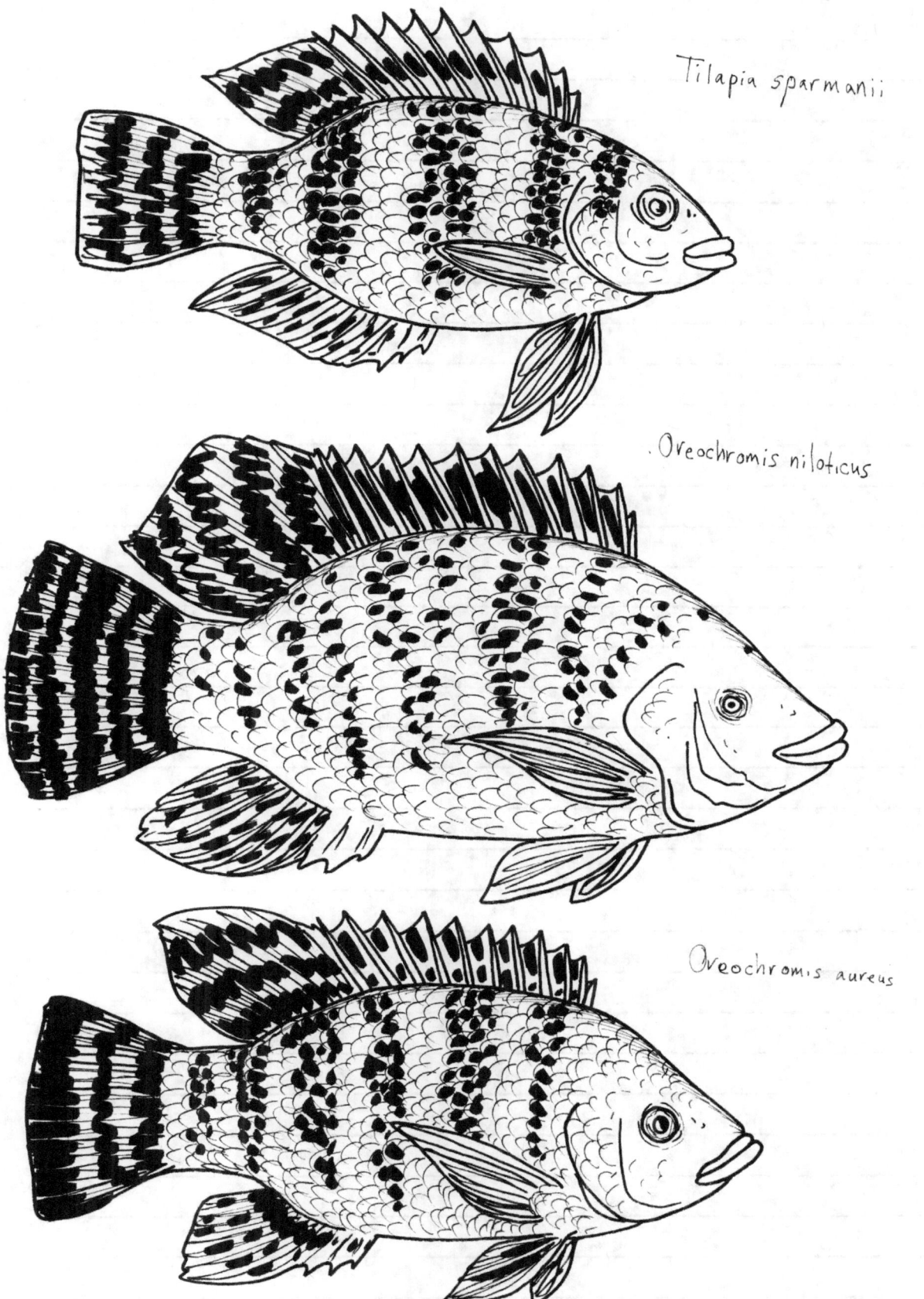

十六

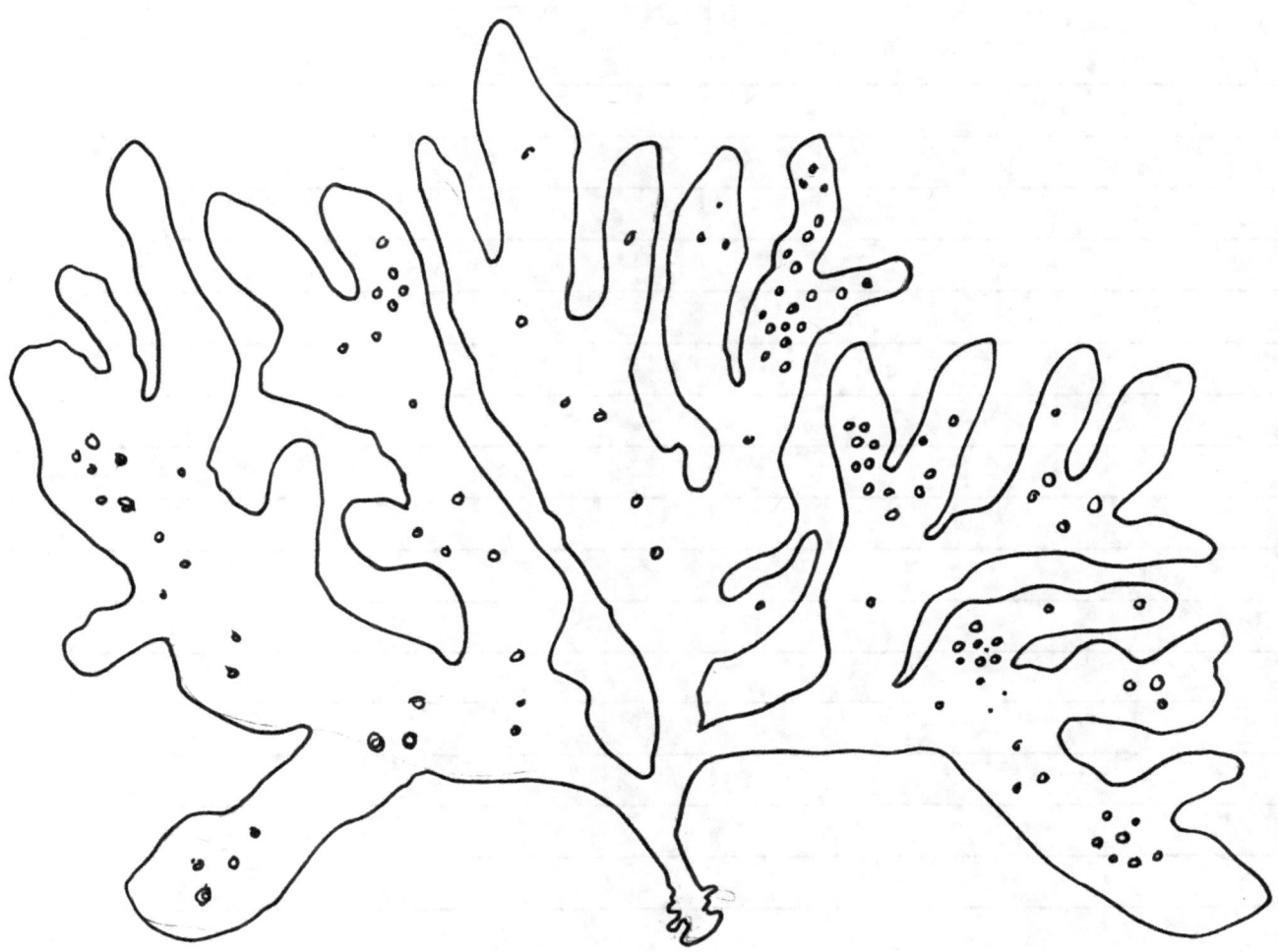

Palmaria palmata

十七

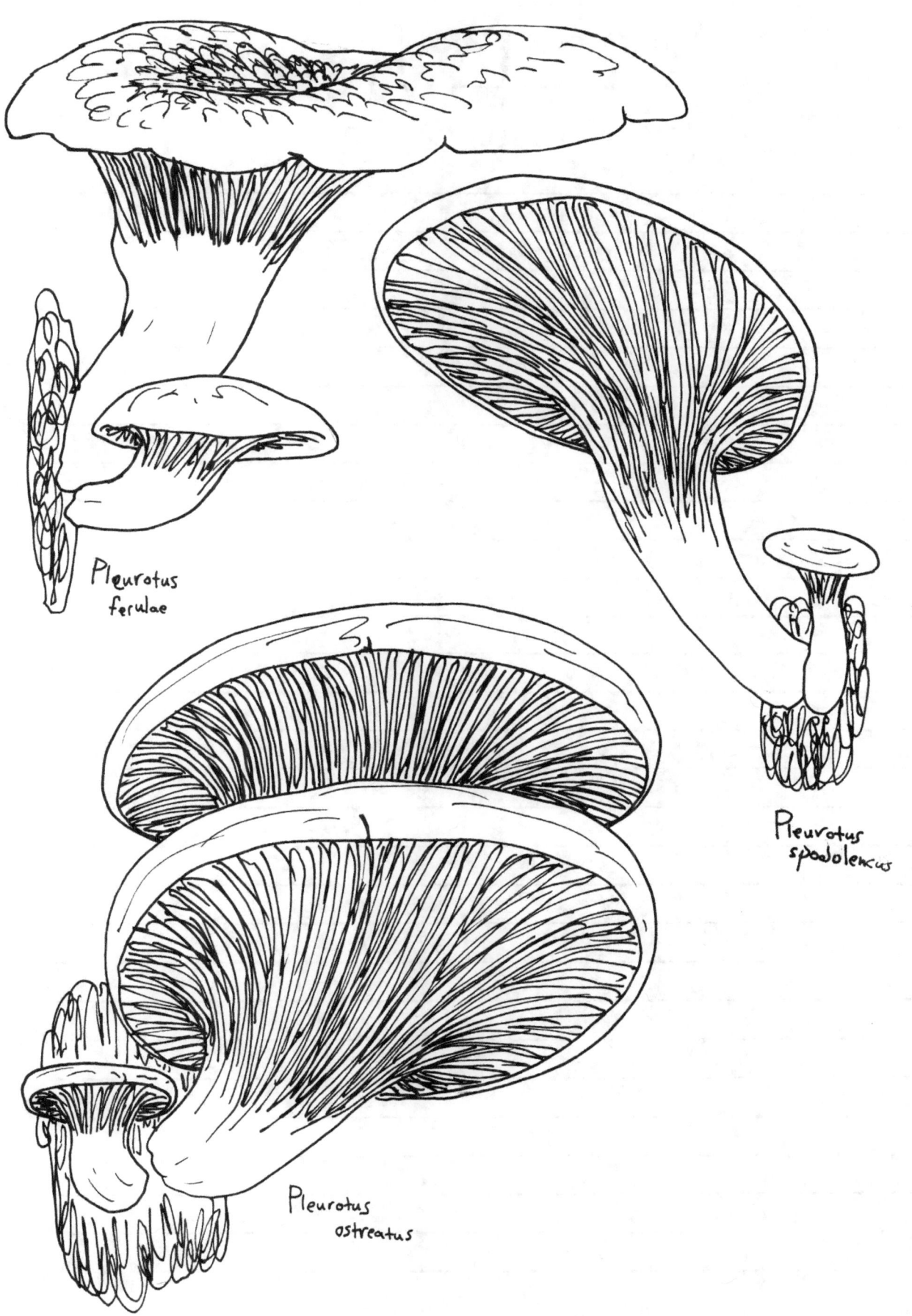

十八

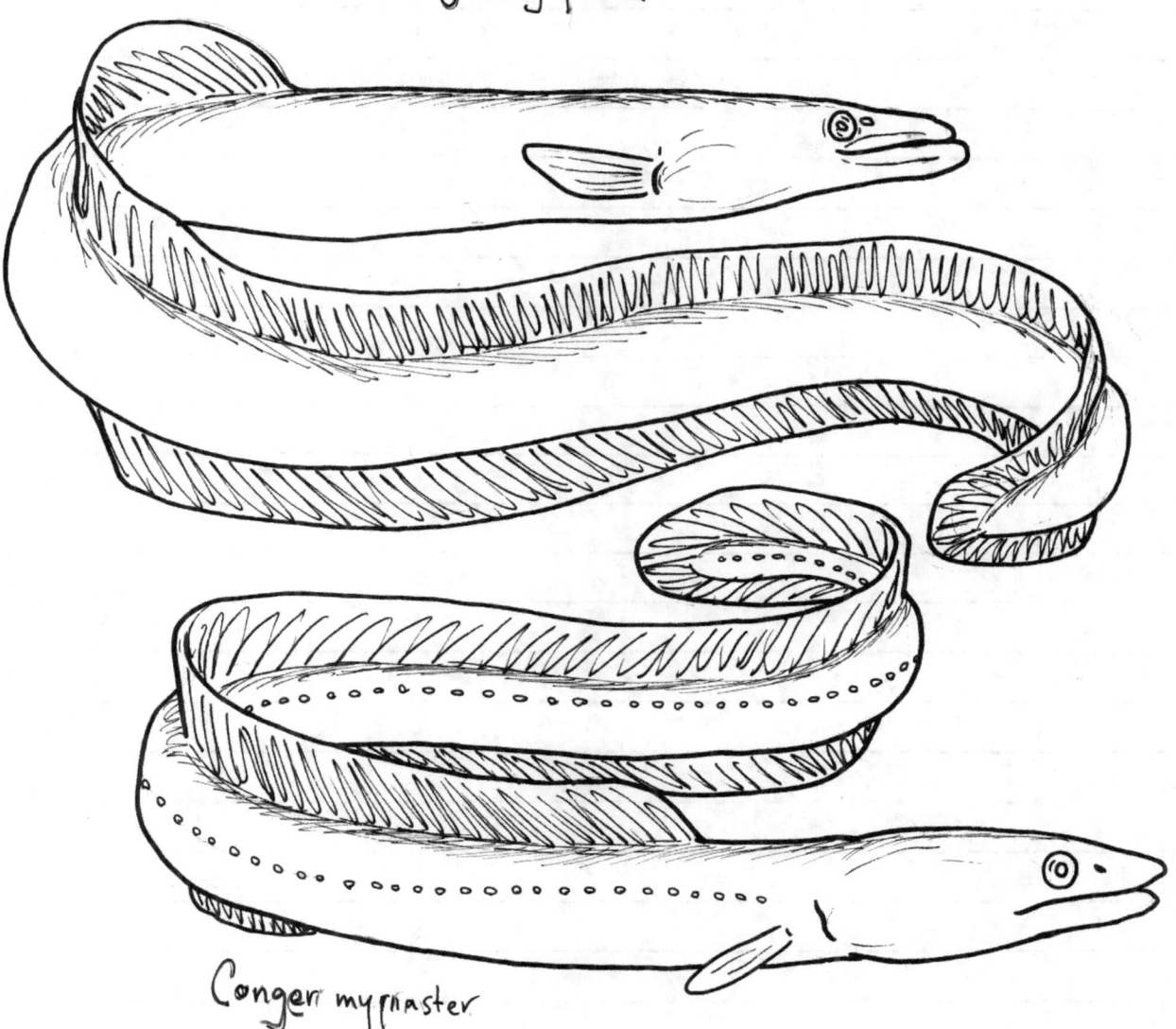

十九

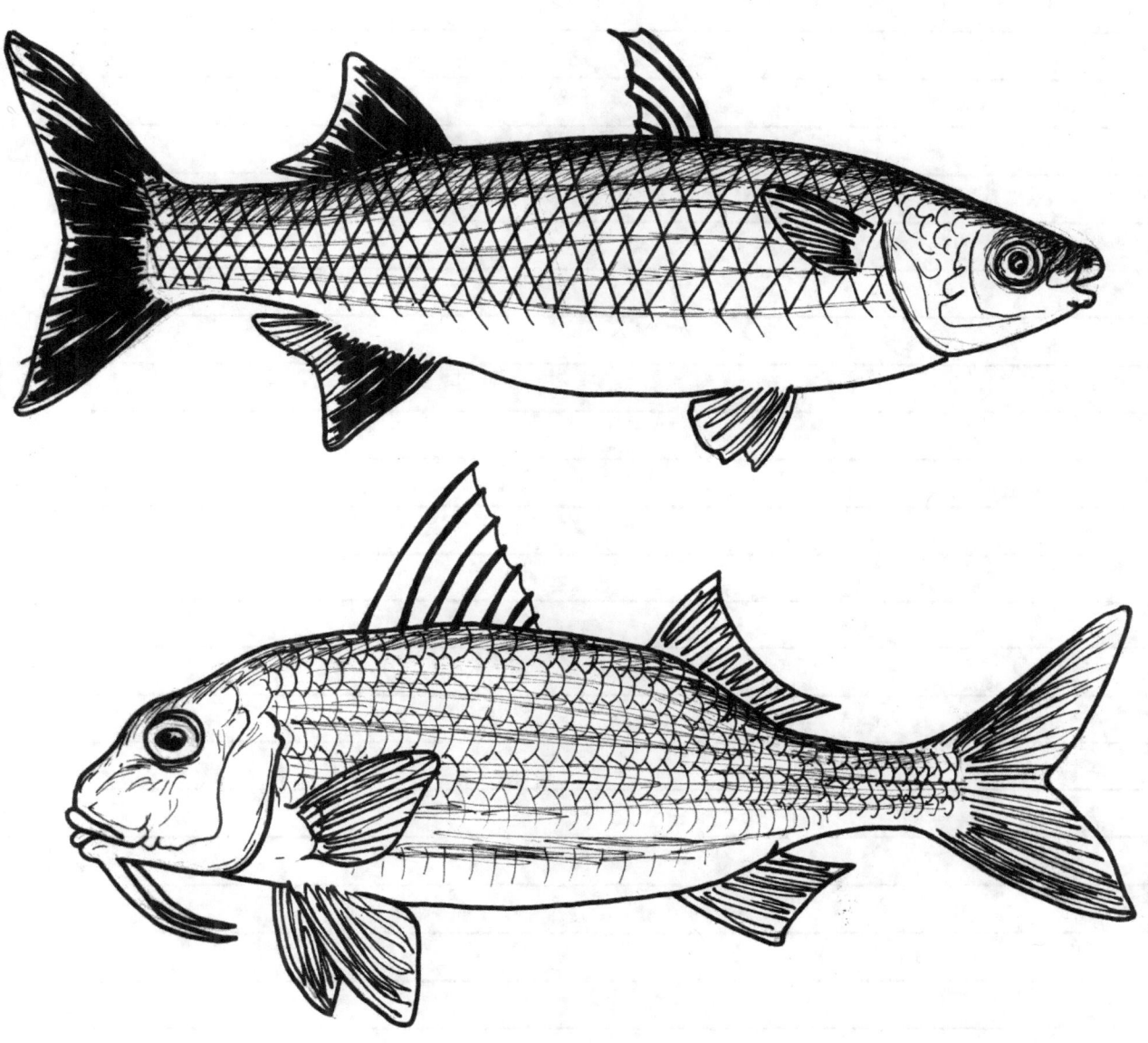

二十

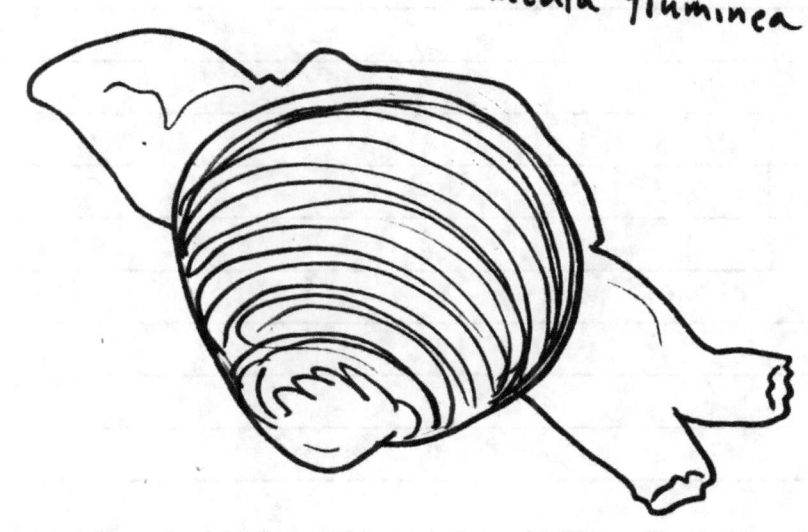

Corbicula fluminea

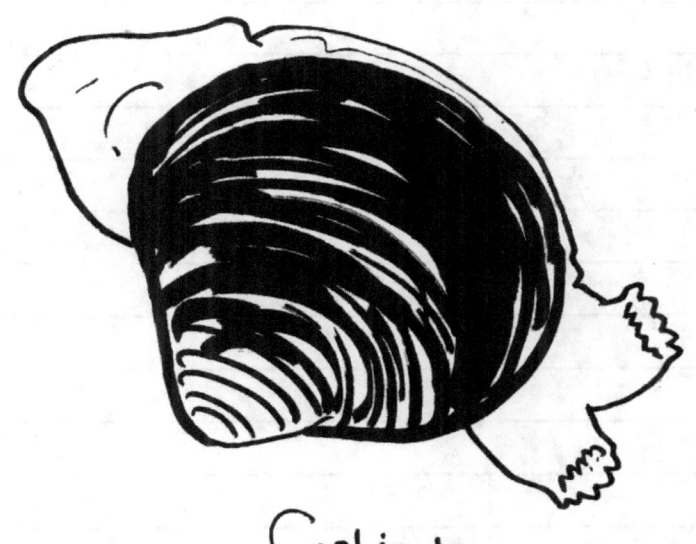

Corbicula japonica

二十一

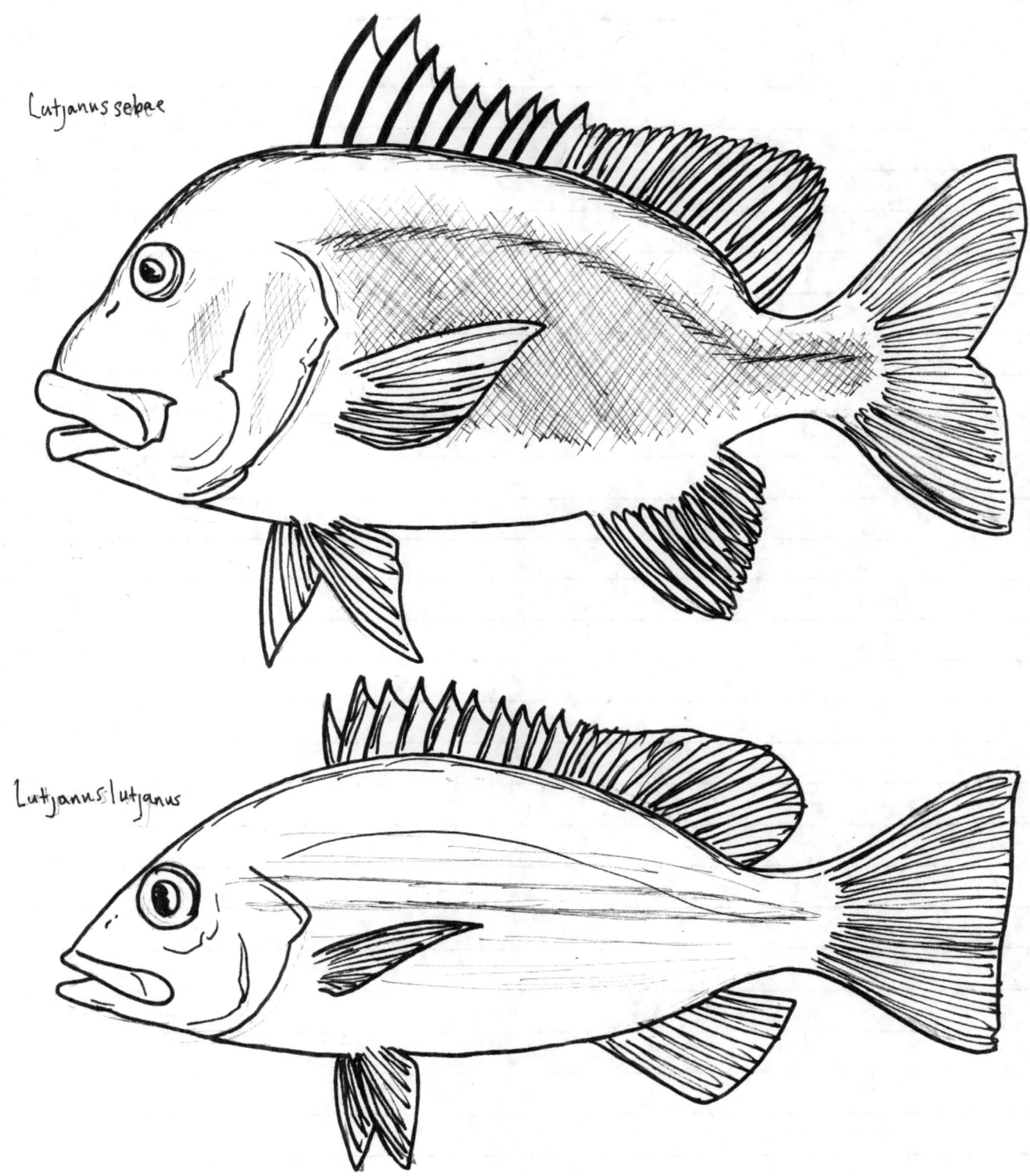

二十二

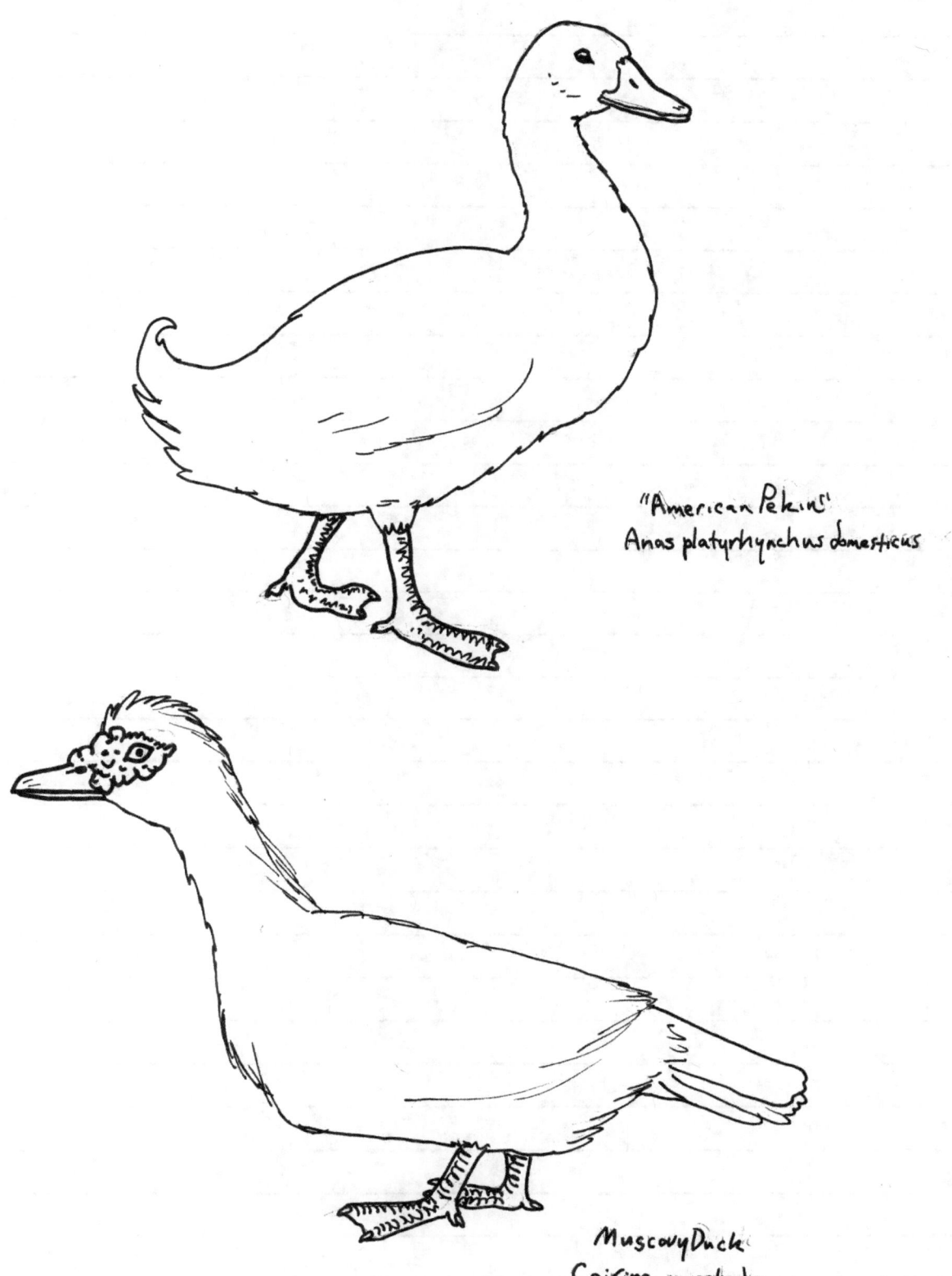

二十三

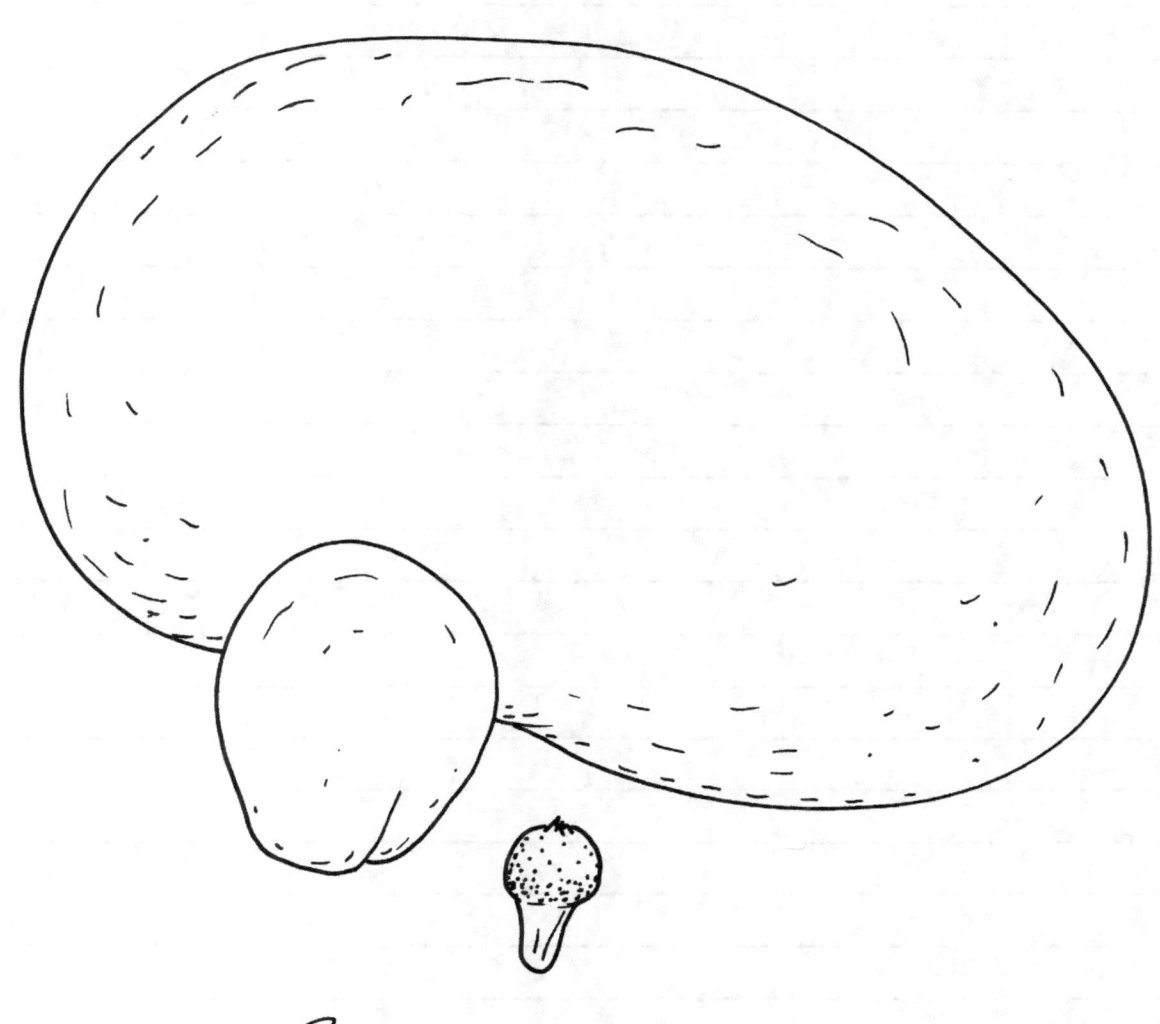

Calvatia gigantea

二十四

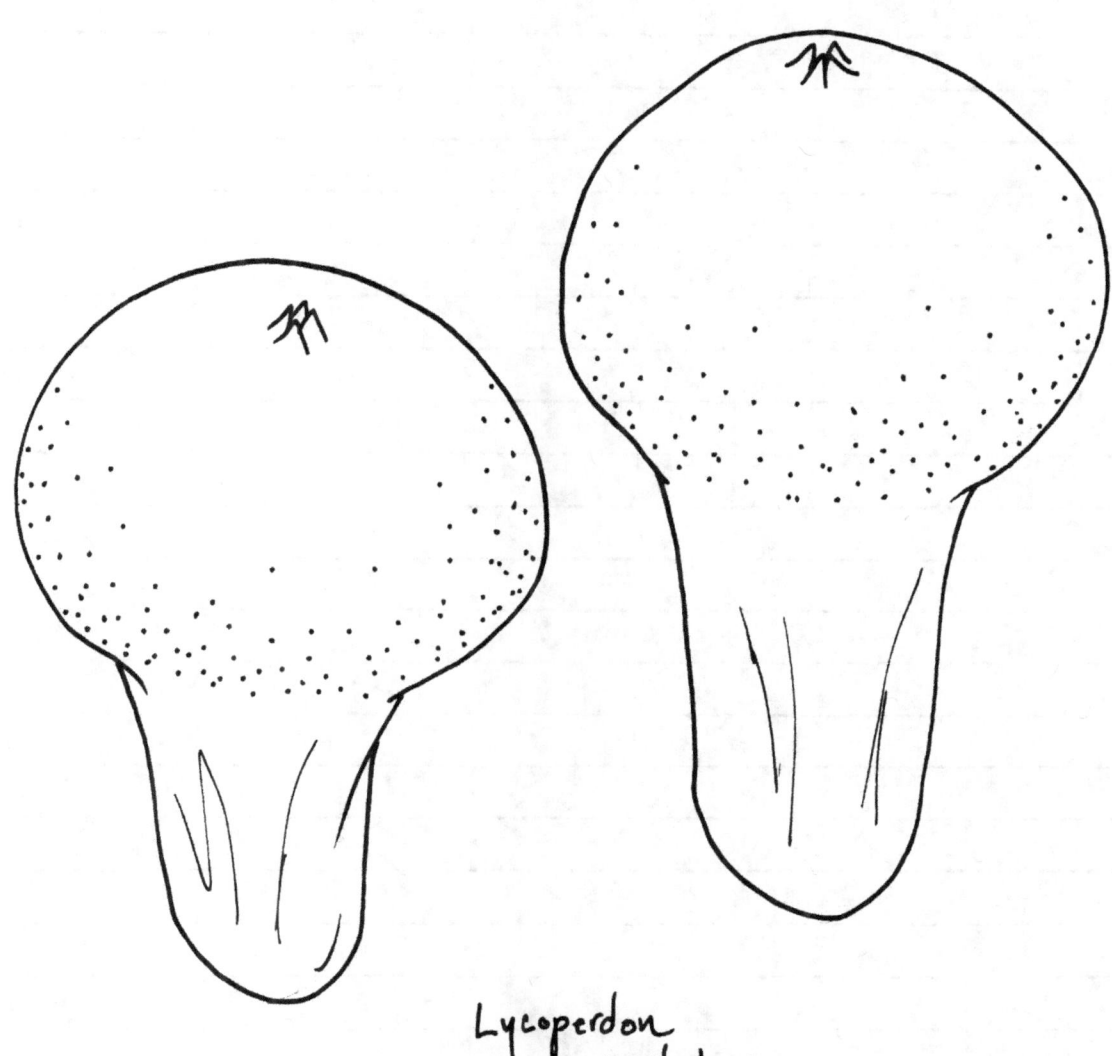

Lycoperdon perlatum

二十五

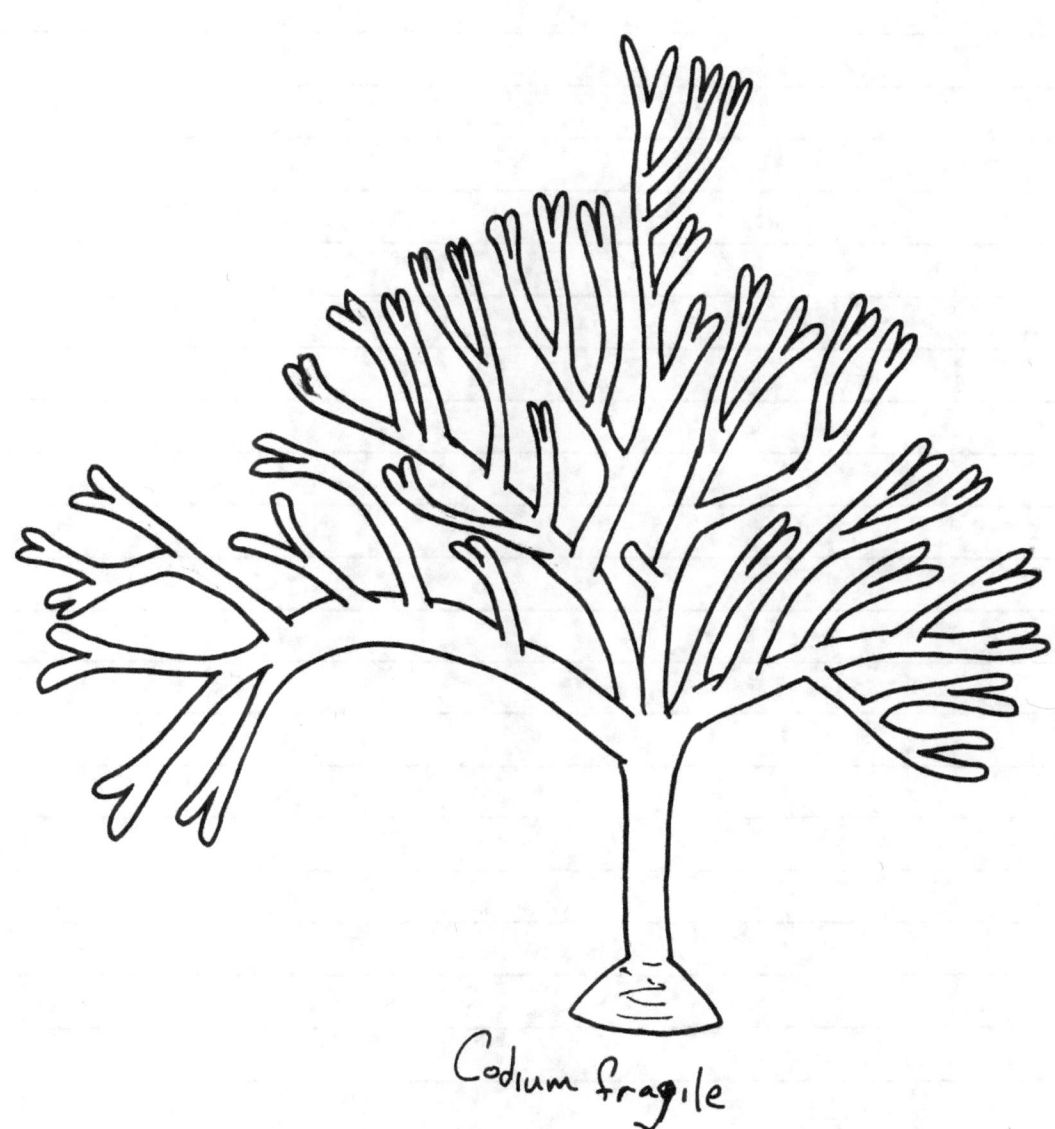

二十六

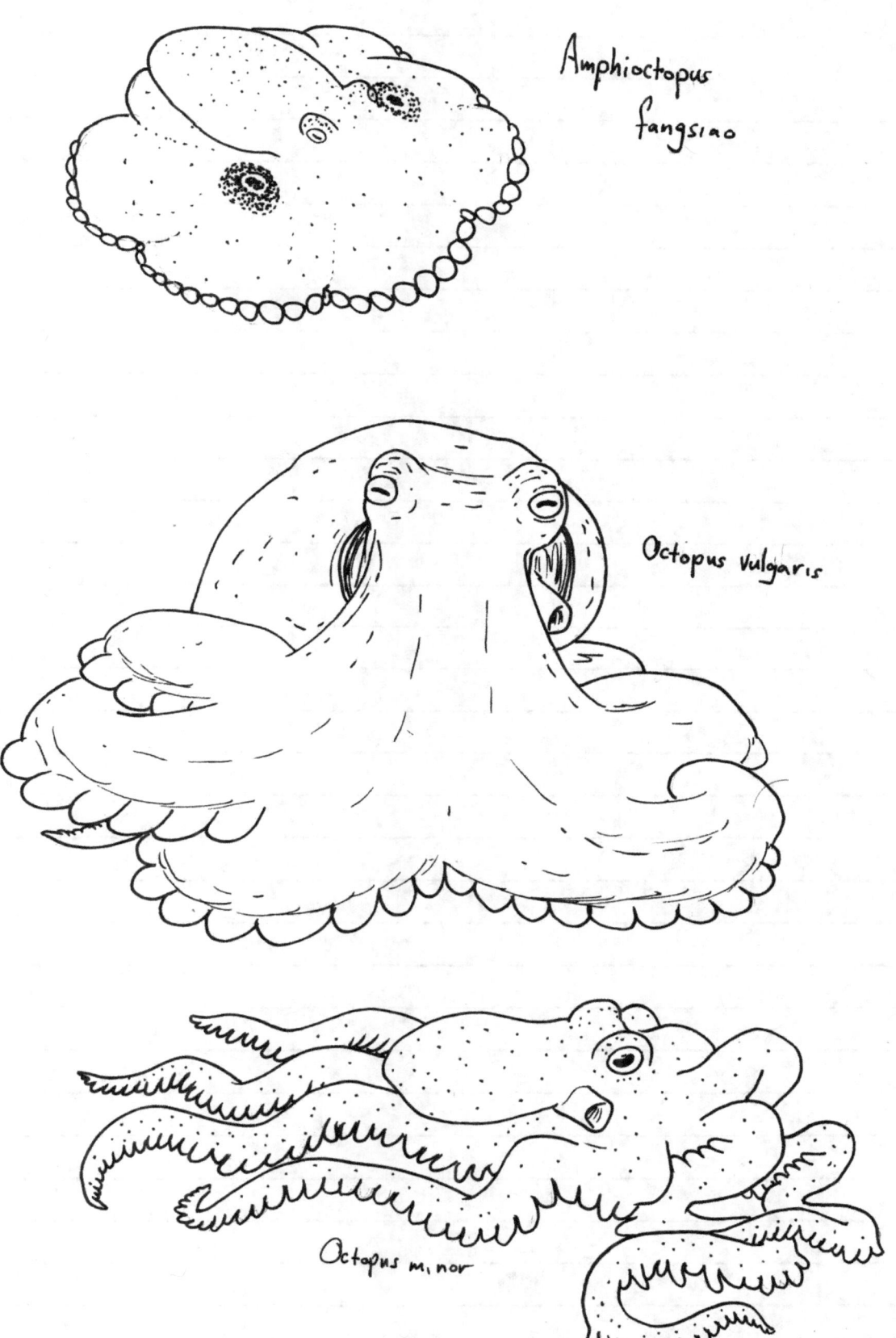

二十七

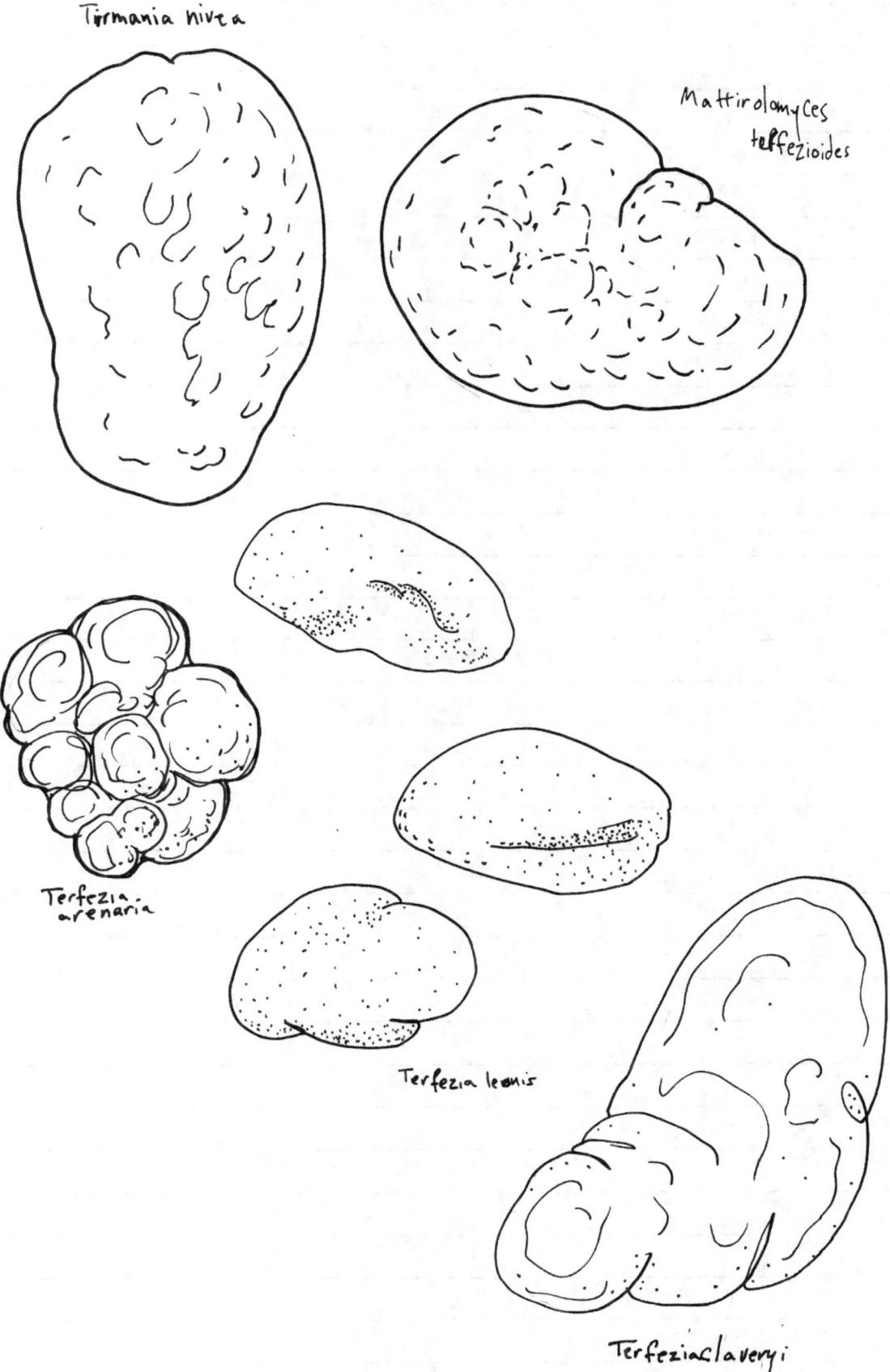

二十八

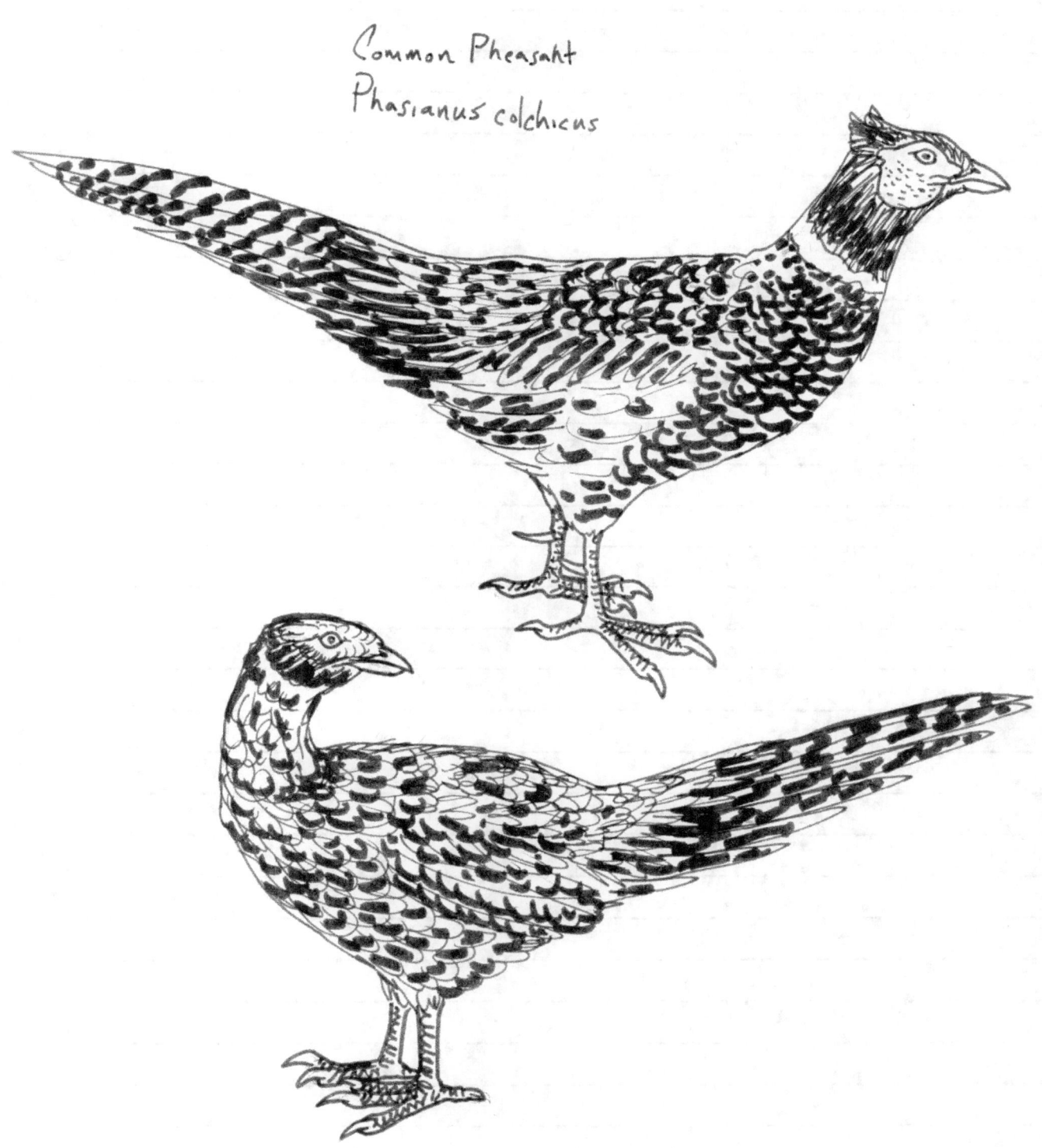

Common Pheasant
Phasianus colchicus

二十九

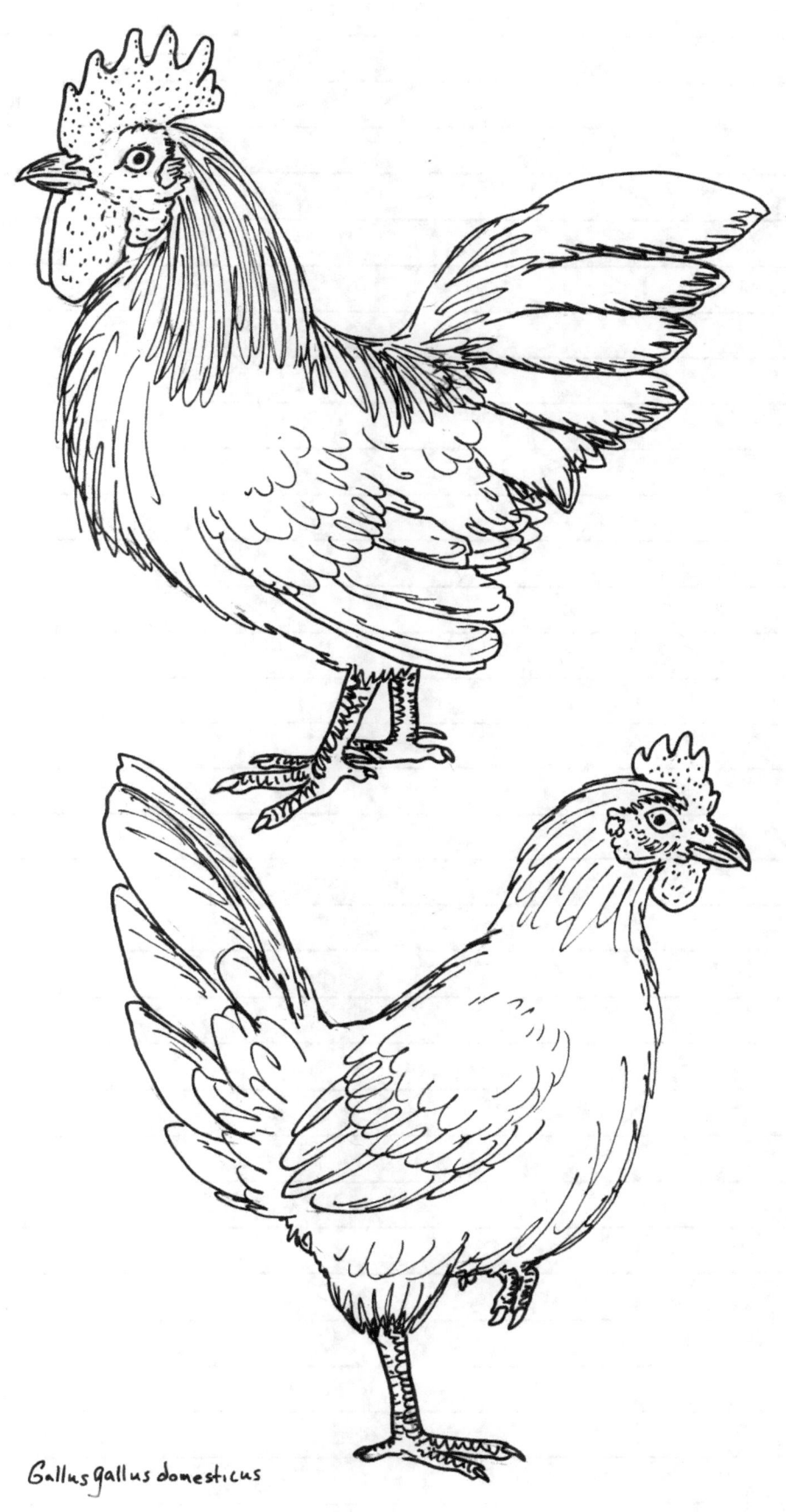

Gallus gallus domesticus

三十

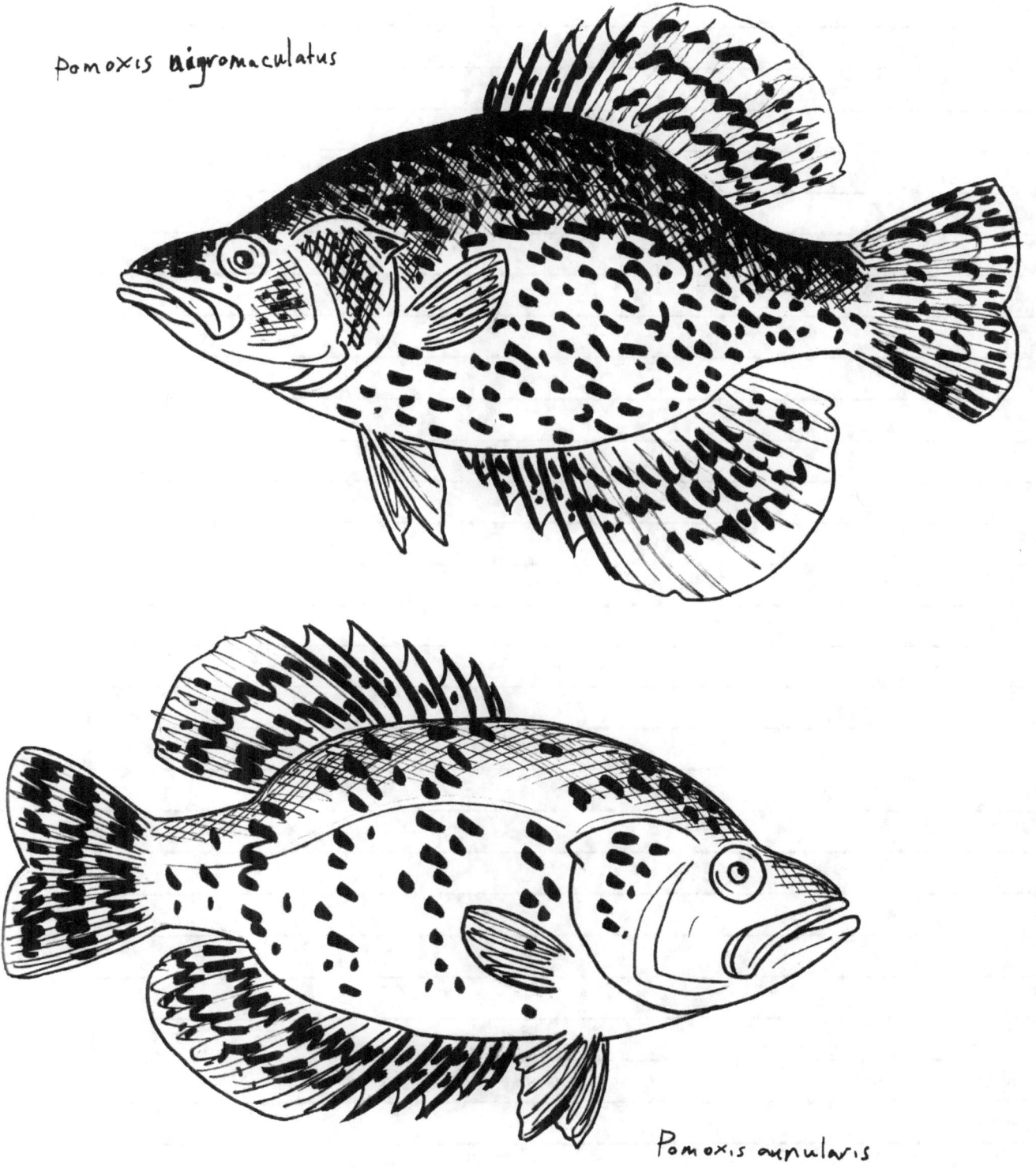

三十一

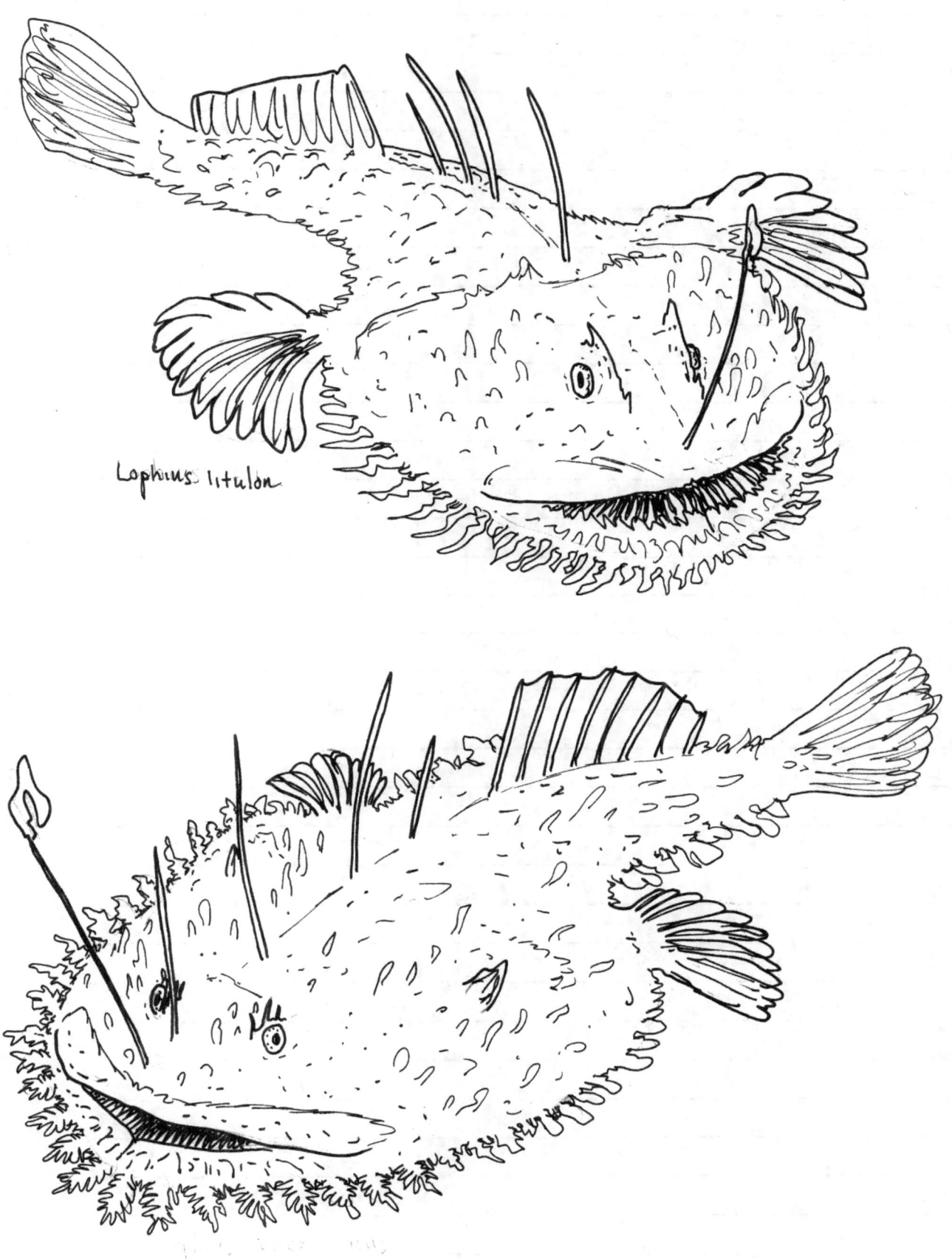

Lophius litulon

Lophius americanus

三十二

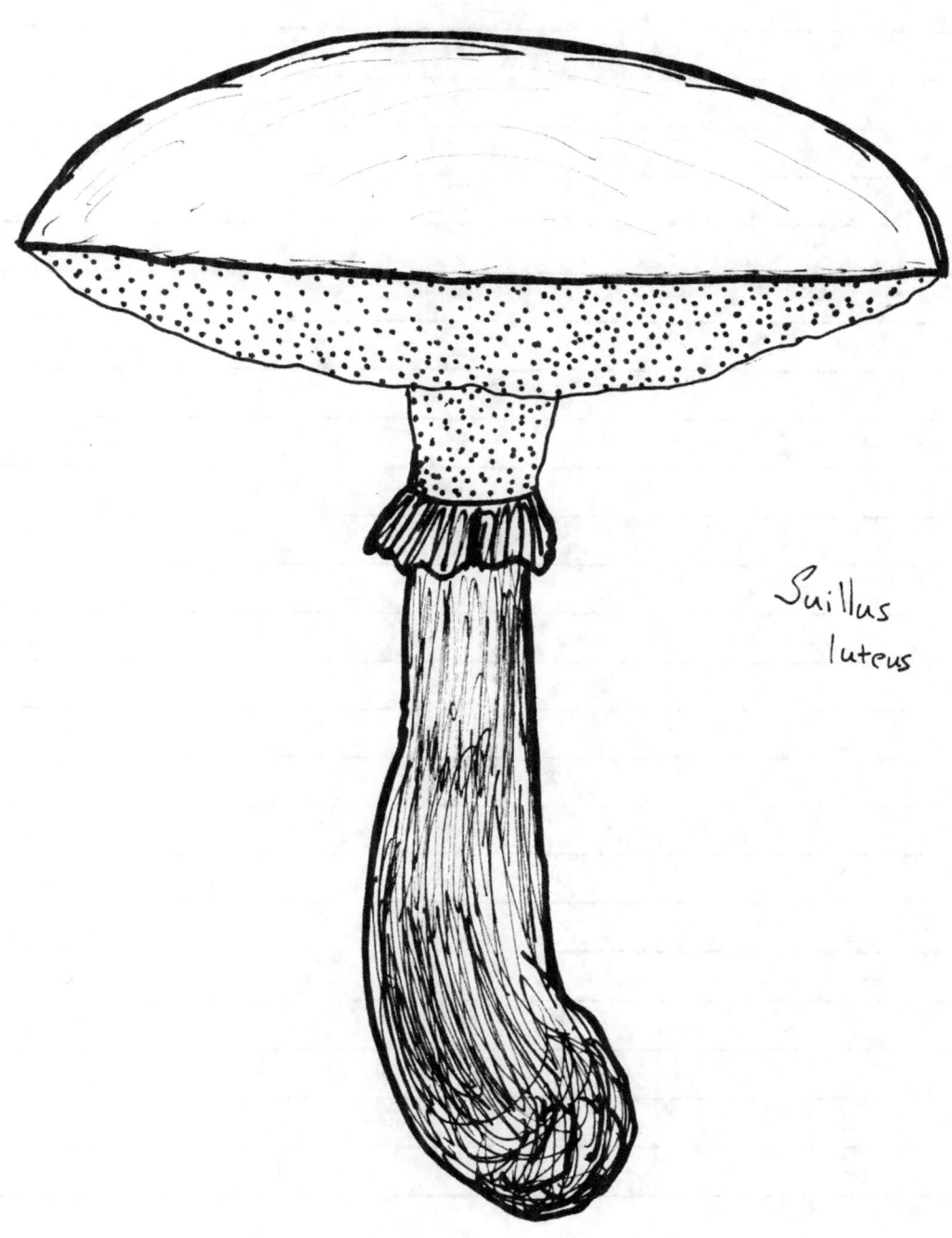

Suillus luteus

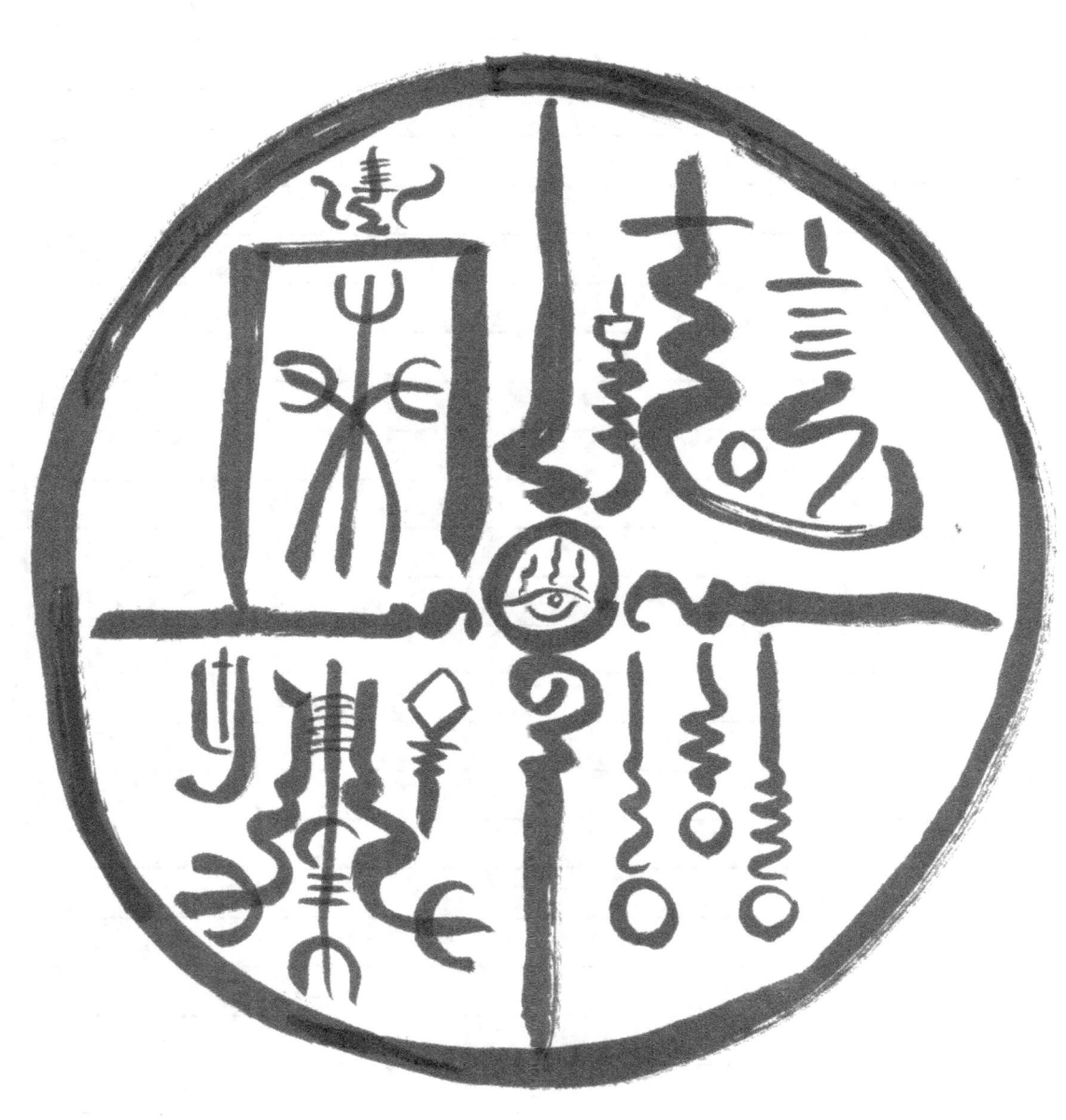

www.ingramcontent.com/pod-product-compliance
Lightning Source LLC
Chambersburg PA
CBHW081425220526
45466CB00008B/2278